LOCOMOTION PAPERS

THE
LITTLE EATON GANGWAY
and DERBY CANAL

by

David Ripley

Loading a canal boat. The crane is lowering a box into a boat. Note the Midland signal box just behind the crane.

THE OAKWOOD PRESS

© David Ripley, 2003
First Edition 1973
Second Edition 1993
Third Edition 2020

ISBN 978-0-85361-746-4

Printed by
P2D Books, 1 Newlands Rd, Westoning, Bedford, MK45 5LD

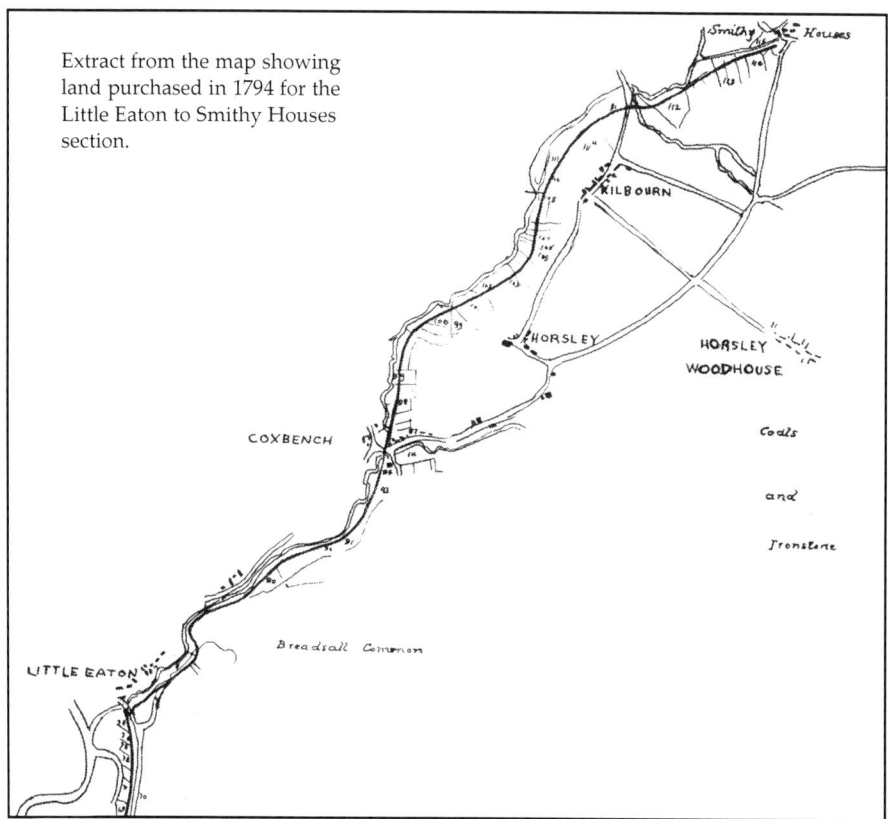

Extract from the map showing land purchased in 1794 for the Little Eaton to Smithy Houses section.

Cover: The wharf at Little Eaton. Stone blocks and short rails guide the gangway to its terminus at the canal basin. The Clock House, which was the wharf agent's office, stands on the other side of the canal. The crane is moving the body of a waggon fom its chassis to the barge in the basin.

Published by
The Oakwood Press, 54-58 Mill Square, Catrine, KA5 6RD
Telephone: 01290 551122   Website: www.stenlake.co.uk

Contents

Preface to Second and Third Editions		4
Introduction		5
One	The River Derwent	7
Two	Early Proposals for the Area	9
Three	The Act	15
Four	Construction of the Line	17
Five	The Railway or Gangway	21
Six	Rolling Stock	31
Seven	The Route	37
Eight	Administration of the Company	51
Nine	Closure	57
Ten	Revival	61

Appendices

One	Major Shareholders of the Derby Canal Company	65
Two	Castings as ordered by the Company	66
Three	Costing for the Company and tonnage carried	67
Four	The Openwoodgate Lines	69
Five	Report from George Stephenson	75
Six	The Derby Canal	77
Seven	Bylaws	79

Acknowledgements	79
Bibliography	80

Preface to the Second Edition

When I wrote the story of the Little Eaton Gangway in 1973, I believed that I had unearthed all the surviving documents that related to it, including the files and minutes of the Derby Canal Company, mine records etc., together with numerous articles in local papers and so forth.

How wrong I was; since then many more documents have come to light, due in many cases to local history classes and societies inspiring their members to further their studies; to these people and many more I am greatly indebted.

Where variations in the spelling of names etc. occurs, I have used the one shown in the base document.

I am also indebted to all those who responded to my letters in the various Derby papers not to mention the editors who kindly published them; to everyone who has helped in any way, may I say, thank you.

David Ripley, 1993

Preface to the Third Edition

In the 10 years since the second edition was published, more and more people have been researching the Derby Canal, in part as a result of the interest shown by the City Council, Local History Groups and Waterways enthusiasts. Following many meetings and a survey the Derby and Sandiacre Canal Society was formed with the objective of re-opening the canal where ever possible and to provide new sections as necessary to form an approx. 25 mile navigable ring with the Erewash & Trent and Mersey Canals. Their website www.derbycanal.org.uk has news on the progress of the restoration and activities of the society. Will any commercial trade be attracted to the network?; it may be that in 20 years time it will partly revert to its original purpose, cheap transportation for the Derby area. During the 1980s – 1990s I gave many talks to various Local History Societies, Women's Institutes and Church groups, some of the talks sponsored by local councils. As a result I received considerable amount of local information from various persons who attended the talks, this in turn has led to the discovery of additional information, much of which is included in this revised edition.

David Ripley, 2003

Introduction

The numerous canals with their associated Railways, Tramways, Gangways (call them what you will), built during the second half of the 18th century are regarded as the first positive steps to provide quick and relatively cheap transport since the days of the Romans.

The Duke of Bridgewater was one of the first to solve the problem of transporting large quantities of goods at a reasonable cost; coal produced at his pits near Worsley almost trebled in price by the time it reached the nearby town of Manchester. With the assistance of a self-educated engineer, James Brindley, he overcame this problem by building a canal, one that was to become the Rennaissance of canal building in Great Britain.

Within a year of his canal, the Bridgewater, opening in 1761, its success was such that factory and mine owners were banding together to promote Bills in Parliament for canals to link the major towns and coalfields, thus kick-starting the Industrial Revolution.

If we look at the position in the Derby area, we find that fuel in the town was expensive, whilst the mines in the Bottle Brook Valley had problems in selling their wares. The late A. Guest looked at the area in detail and found that the forest cover which had once provided fuel in the form of charcoal no longer existed, most of it having been used to convert iron ore into bar-iron. It is said that eight young birch trees each containing approx 5.125 cu. ft of timber would have been needed to convert sufficient iron ore into one ton of bar-iron. The first Derbyshire coke fuelled iron furnace was erected around 1780 and used coals from Marhay Colliery and ironstone from Morley Park.

All-weather roads were not available, navigation on the rivers was hindered by shallows, weirs and fords. Coal shortages occurred in the lower Trent Valley, when due to problems of transit along the Don and Trent rivers there was none or very little coal arriving from the Yorkshire coalfields. Yet profits at the collieries in the Bottle Brook Basin were meagre, the combined profits of Denby and Robey Fields Collieries for the first six months of 1785 only amounted to £7 5s. 4½d. [£7.27].
Derby needed a canal.

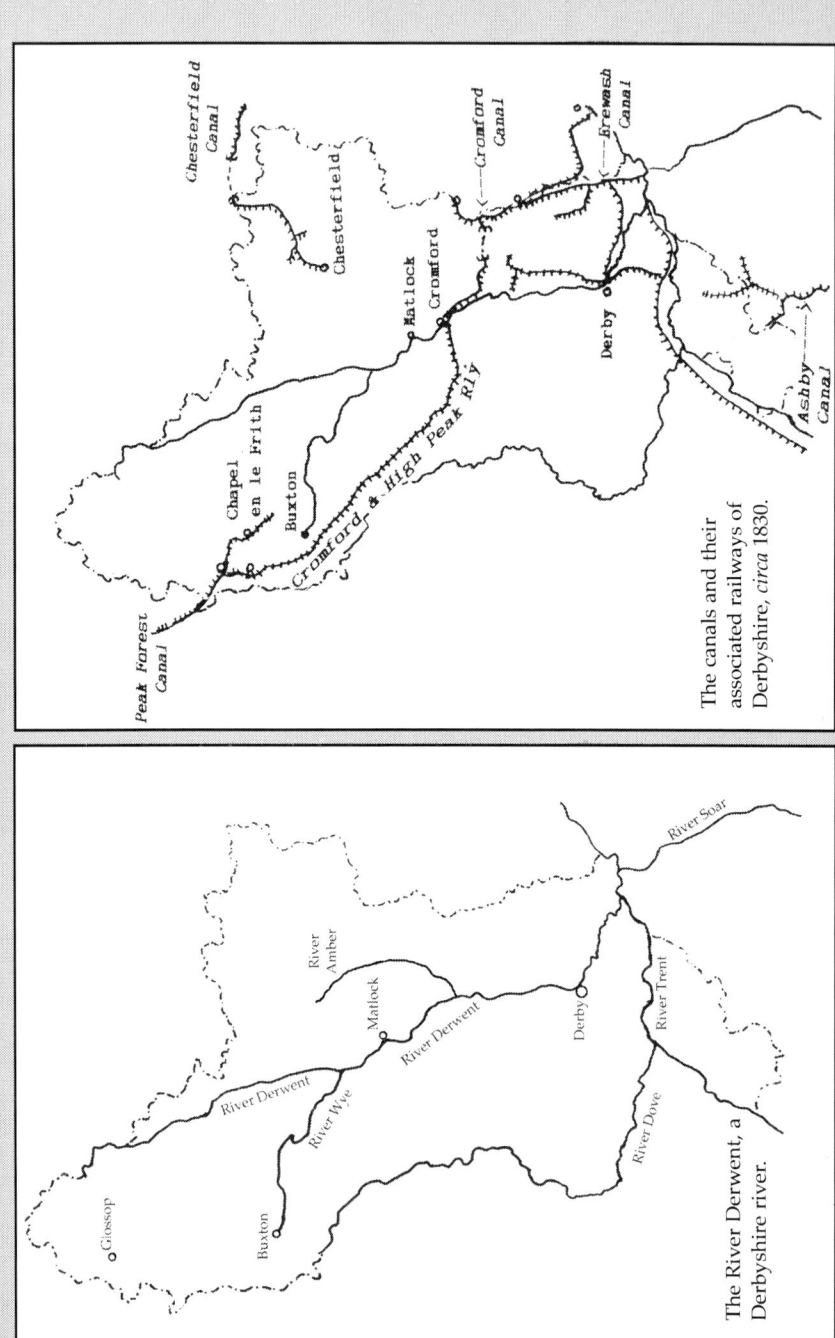

The canals and their associated railways of Derbyshire, circa 1830.

The River Derwent, a Derbyshire river.

Chapter One

The River Derwent

The River Derwent is a Derbyshire river in the true sense of the word, it rises near the northern boundary of the County in the Peak District, is fed by the Wye, the Amber and several other minor rivers as it winds south, passing through Derby until it joins the River Trent at Great Wilne.

The river had served the town of Derby for over 500 years (longer if we include the use of it by the Romans) a charter granted by King John in 1204 gave the townsmen the right to use 'Darwent, Navigable from ancient times'. Despite the Charter, mill owners built weirs, which obstructed traffic and so coupled with a shortage of water in dry seasons (which occurred frequently in the 17th century), led to a series of Bills being placed before Parliament to improve the navigation. Due to the powerful opposition to these Bills mounted by the Mill Owners and the Corporation of Nottingham, the former not wishing to lose their mill water supplies, and the latter seeking to maintain their position as the main port on the Trent, the Bills failed to reach the Statute Books.

One Bill which faired better than its predecessors was submitted in 1719, it received the Royal Assent (5.Geo.I) in April 1720. It provided for 10 miles of the River Derwent from its junction with the River Trent at Great Wilne up to Derby to be made navigable. The works when completed improved the navigation, but the problem of water shortages during drought periods caused problems. The local papers were soon remarking that boats were once more stranded on the shoals for weeks on end. It became very evident that the river was not a true highway, its use being restricted to the winter and spring, as these were the main periods when one could be sure of ample water to enable navigation.

A further problem occurred when heavy snowfalls in the Peak District caused flooding due to rapid thaws. The floodwaters carried debris down stream, silting up certain sections, scouring others and eroding the banks.

Several dry summers occurred in the mid-1700s, this with the success of canals which had being built caused a new Bill to be to be submitted to Parliament for a canal. The Derwent Navigation Trustee had a clause added to the proposed Bill, the clause providing for the canal company to purchase the Derwent Navigation as soon as the canal was built.

The Bill reached the statute book and under the terms of the clause, the canal company paid £3,996 for the shares of the Navigation. Thus in 1794 the Navigation ceased as a separate authority.

Long Bridge and weir, *circa* 1905. The canal crossed the River Derwent on the upstream side of the bridge which acted as a towpath. Water was supplied from the Sandiacre branch to the Swarkestone line by a siphon under the weir.

Part of the navigable section of the River Derwent seen from Derwent Bridge.

Chapter Two

Early Proposals for the Area

James Brindley in 1771, whilst working on the Trent and Mersey Canal, had proposed that a canal be built to link the Trent and Mersey with another canal that he was engineer for, the Chesterfield Canal. He proposed that the link would utilize the Derwent, Trent, Amber and Erewash Valleys, tapping the coalfields of Derbyshire, Nottingham and South Yorkshire as well as the rich farmlands through which it would run. Had it been built, it is doubtful if the Erewash, Nottingham, Cromford or Derby canals would have been built in their final form, that is if they would have been built at all. Short connecting canals similar to the Nutbrook would have serviced towns like Derby. A bold idea doomed by the lack of foresight of the landowners, in particular those with large Estates and fancy houses, the opposition once more of the Nottingham Corporation and others with a vested interest in the River Trent.

If it had been built it would have provided a safe route from West Stockwith, where the Chesterfield Canal joined the River Trent south to Wilden Ferry on the River Trent, avoiding over 70 miles of a river which was mainly tidal and liable to floods.

Nearly 20 years were to pass before there was any action in promoting a canal to serve Derby occurred, 20 years which had seen the building of the Erewash Canal [Act 17 Geo.III, 30th April, 1777, opened by Dec.1779] and the start of the Cromford Canal, [Act 20 Geo.III 1789]. William Jessop estimated the total tonnage on the River Trent in 1790 to be 89,950 tons, of which dues were paid at Trent Bridge on some 76,000 tons and the balance was paid at Newark.

The *Derby Mercury* of 15th September, 1791, carried not one item, but two, on schemes to link Derby to the River Trent. The first was a report of a meeting held the previous day at the Bell Inn, Derby, where a canal was proposed to run from the Trent and Mersey Canal at Swarkestone to Derby, whilst the second item was a notice of a proposed canal from the Trent and Mersey at Shardlow to Derby, this having the support of both the Erewash and Trent and Mersey companies.

It was nearly 12 months before we hear of a further meeting (August 1792) being held, at which a committee was elected to investigate the most suitable route for a canal, to benefit not only Derby, but also Denby, Newall and Swadlincote.

Benjamin Outram was commissioned to carry out a survey and report back to the committee. He lost no time in carrying out his survey and he was able to report to a meeting held in September, that, as a result of his

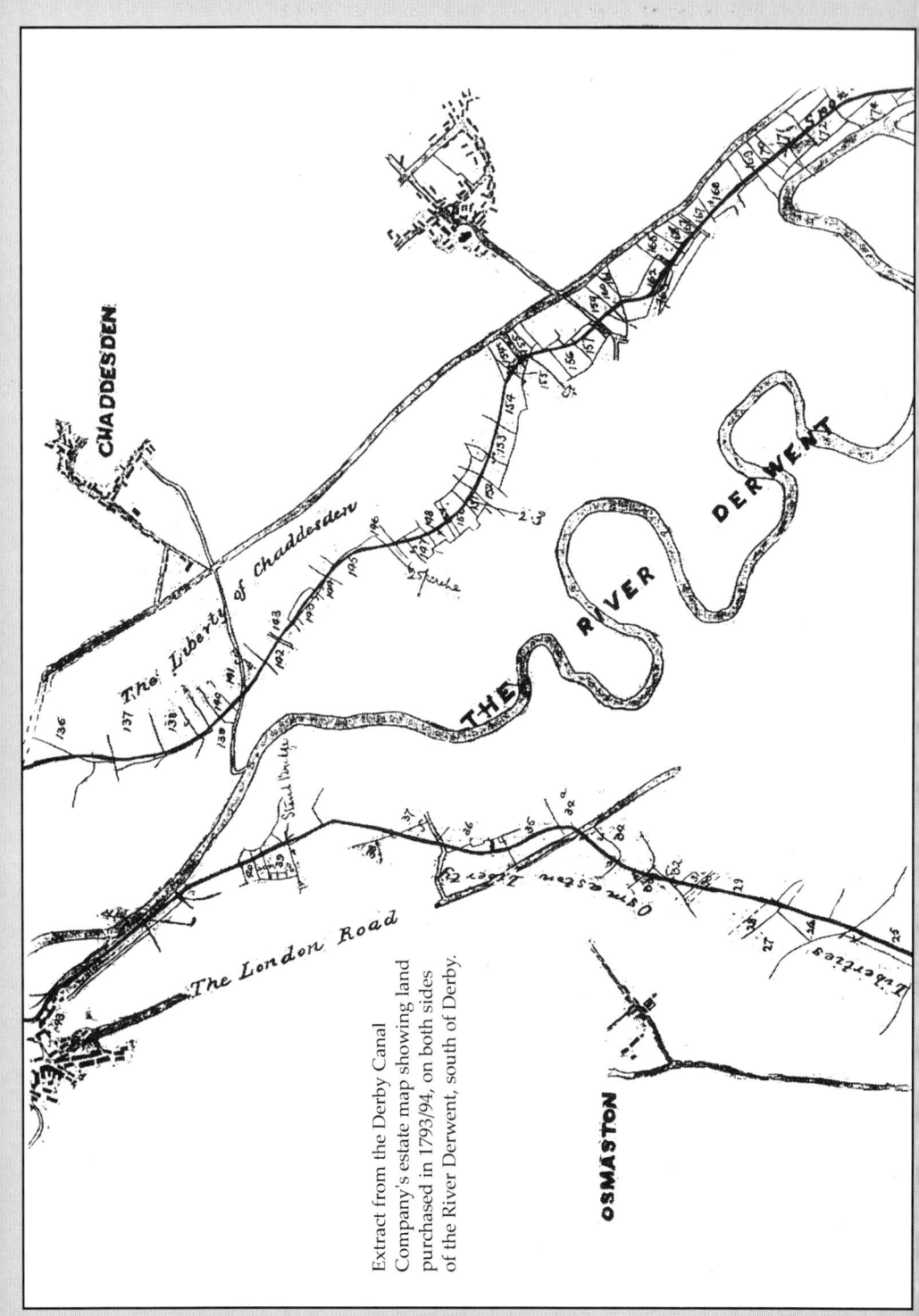

Extract from the Derby Canal Company's estate map showing land purchased in 1793/94, on both sides of the River Derwent, south of Derby.

survey he proposed a canal with a main line from the Trent and Mersey at Swarkestone to Derby and Denby and a branch from Derby to the Erewash at Sandiacre. This was the most useful route with regard to both traffic and populace.

The committee was not fully in agreement with Outram's proposals and asked William Jessop to comment on the proposed route. In a paper dated 3rd November, 1792, addressed to the Chairman of Subscribers to the intended Derby Canal, Jessop confirmed the major part of Outram's survey, with the suggestion that the canal should terminate at Little Eaton instead of at Denby.

[NB: The letter has been copied from the original, the spellings and use of capitals etc. follow the original, the only changes are that the old form of 's' which resembled an 'f' have been changed to modern form.]

Sir,
I have viewed the several Lines of Canal set out by Mr.Outram, and have examined his Estimates of effecting them... The line from the Erewash Canal, passes through Ground exceedingly favourable to the Intention; the Benefits which will accrue from the Facility of getting Lime, will make ample amends to the Occupiers for the Loss of some valuable Land; and there are many Villages in its Way that will be conveniently accommodated with Coal and other Articles.

The Line from Swarkstone, tho' not quite so smooth as the other, is not to be complained of; I believe Mr. Outram on his re-surveying it, will improve his former Track, particularly from the Fields North-West of Chellaston, he will find better Ground for the Purpose over the South-East End of Sinfin Moor.

Instead of joining the Grand Trunk Canal at Cuttle Bridge, it appears most advisable to join it above the Lock next above the Bridge; and passing on that Canal about twelve chains, and descending by three Locks, a very short Line will meet the River Trent immediately above Swarkstone Bridge.

It would be practicable to pass over the Canal; but it would have a very unfriendly Appearance. I cannot suppose that the Proprietors of the Grand Trunk can object to an Union with it: The considerable Quantity of Lime now brought by Land Carriage to the Canal, proves that much more may hereafter be brought by Water; and the Increaſe of Trade that always attende Collateral Extensions, will probably more than compensate for the loss of Tonnage on a few miles in Length; and surely a canal that was meant to be a public Good should nott be converted into an Evil, by becoming as Obstruction to others, instead of expanding its own Utility.

The lines from Denby and Smalley Collieries are practicable on either of the ways that Mr. Outram has projected; and if made navigable all the Way, may be amply supplied with Water by a Reservoir.

But I am clearly of Opinion, that the most eligible Scheme will be that of a Canal from Derby to Little Eaton; and from thence Railways to the Collieries,

An engraving from *The Land We Live In* by Charles Knight. It shows the canal entering the River Derwent, on its branch to the river, downstream from St Mary's Bridge.

– If those Railways, which should be of Cast Iron, are substantially laid upon Stone Foundations, and ascend on a regular Acclivity from Eaton to the Collieries, one Horse will easily draw down two Waggons with two Tons on each; and empty, they will as easily be drawn up again, as I understand the Ascent is only one sixth of an Inch in a Yard of length; these Waggons may be drawn on to Boats and conveyed to Derby, and may be so constructed as to be carried into the Town without unloading. – Putting Tonnage out of the Question they cannot be carried so cheap by a Canal the whole length as by the proposed Railways. The only seeming Objection would be the Inconvenience to back Carriage; but as little Lime could go beyond Eaton in any Way, at a lesser Price than that which is now brought by Land Carriage to that Neighbourhood, there could hardly be any Thing else that would pay for the extraordinary Expenditure of Twelve Thousand Pounds.

Respecting the Union of the Canals by crossing the River at Derby, it is clear that a saving of £4,000, may be made by the Way, Proposed by Mr. Outram of erecting a Weir, and passing into and out of the River by Locks, instead of crossing by an Aqueduct; and his mode of supplying the Canals with Water I think is unexceptional.

EARLY PROPOSALS FOR THE AREA

Floods will obstruct the Passage of the River, but it will not be much inconvenient, as Floods in the Derwent quickly subside. – Coals will always have access to the Town; and in general or continued Floods when Lime Boats might be stopped. They would also be stopped by the Trent at Swarkstone, as would Boats coming from Gainsbro'.

Mr. Outram's Prices of Estimation are in general very sufficient; when his Surveys are completed some Corrections may be made.

My Opinion has been asked of the Scheme in Agitation from Shardlow to Nottingham with a Branch to Derby;

If the Canals already described were wholly out of the Question, this might be the next best Thing for Derby; but for any other Purpose I think it ineligible. I have Reason for believing that few boats will use the line parallel to the Trent, if they are not compelled to do so; for as the Trent Navigation is generally as good above Nottingham as below; the Boatman will hardly like to be deprived of the use of their Sails (which frequently enable them to move with more Expedition and Facility than can upon any Canal obstructed by Locks and Bridges) and pay a Guinea and Half per Voyage extraordinary into the Bargin.

The only material Recommendation of it, is its avoiding Nottingham Bridge; but this might be effected in another way at a comparatively trifling Expense.

So far as this Scheme might operate in diverting the Trade from the River Trent, so far it would do a public Injury; as it would deprive the Managers of it, or part of the Means of continuing the gradual Improvement of that River.

Upon the whole it is indisputable that the three Lines of Canal – from the Erewash – from Derby and its Vicinity – and from Swarkstone – will effectually secure to the Town and Neighbourough of Derby the Articles of Coal and Lime cheap and certain; and to the general Commerce of the Town, they will be proportionally useful.

I am, Sir,
Your most obedient Servant,
W. Jessop
NEWARK, Nov 3d. 1792

Outram made a comprehensive survey and in the main adopted the recommendations of Jessop, the canal across Sinfin Moor, a railway instead of a canal to Denby being the main changes to his original plan.

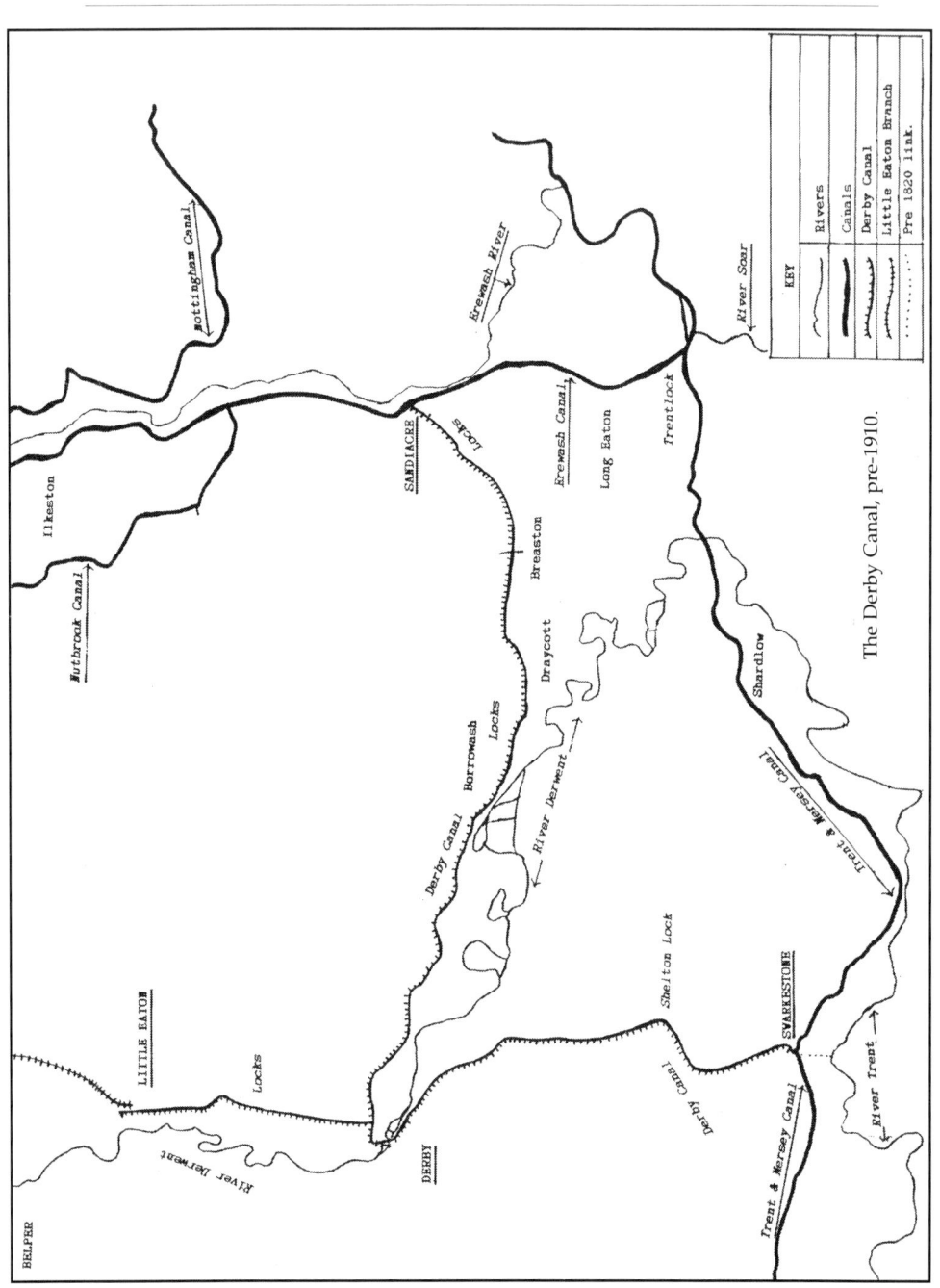

The Derby Canal, pre-1910.

Chapter Three

The Act

After receiving Jessop's report, a committee was formed to formulate a Bill to present to Parliament. They had the survey re-checked and plans drawn up to be deposited with the Clerk to the Peace for the County of Derbyshire.

It was proposed that the share capital should be £60,000 comprising 600 shares of £100 each and that additional powers would allow them to raise a further sum of £30,000, also dividends were to be limited to 8 per cent.

At this point we must pause to consider why a canal and railway were needed. Derby in 1790 was listed as the 45th town in England with a population of 13,000. A look at the geological map for the area reveals that the proposed line of the railway would cut across the junction of the Midland Coal Field with the Millstone Grit series of rocks, the coal coming to the surface in several places where, at that time, both drift mines and bell pits were in being worked. Also both the canal and railway passed through good agricultural land.

Thus the general objects as stated in the Act were correct, these were:

> Supply of Derby with coals, building stone, Gypsum and other articles.
> Export of coals from the Denby Area.
> Export of manufactured goods, cheese and other agricultural produce from the Vale of the Derwent and Bottle Rivers.

The preamble to the Act as deposited reads:

> An Act for making and maintaining a navigable canal from the River Trent at or near Swarkestone Bridge to and through the Borough of Derby to Little Eaton, with a cut out of the said canal in or near the said Borough to join the Erewash Canal near Sandiacre: and for making Railways from such canal to several collieries in the Parishes or Liberties of Denby, Horsley and Smally, all in the County of Derby.

While page 4 of the Act sets out the reasons for the railways:

> And to make and maintain a Rail or Waggon Way or Stone Road for the conveyance of Coal, Iron, Ironstone, Lead Ore, Limestone and other articles in carriages or vehicles constructed for that purpose, from the termination of the said canal at Little Eaton aforesaid or from some places near thereto or near a certain place in the Parish of Denby, called Smithy Houses.

Further clauses in the Act were to mitigate losses by landowners and others who were likely to be affected by the canal. One of these clauses as previously mentioned provided for the canal company to purchase from the owners of the Derwent River Navigation, 'Their rights, wharves, and warehouses for £3,696'.

An Indenture dated the 27th March, 1794 between the River Derwent Navigation and the Derby Canal Company still exists; from this document the total of £3,696 was paid to 'shareholders' of the Navigation according to their rights. They were-

Samuel ffox	£1,386 (spelling as per document)
Thomas Evans	£462
William Evans	£462
Samuel Godfin	£202
William Streton	£924
Thomas Carter	£130
Samuel Sheppardson	£130

Another clause provide that 'Railways to be made to Horley Colliery if required by Phillip, Earl of Chesterfield, the rails to be of good and sound Heart or Oak of the dimensions of 6 in. x 4 in.' In addition all railways over Lord Chesterfield's land were to be fenced.

Further clauses related to the limitation on dividends (up to 8 per cent, after which the money had to go to a reserve balance to reduce tolls) and for the canal company to allow up to 5,000 tons of coal a year to be carried toll-free to Derby for the use of the poor, one way of reducing the 'poor rate'.

Despite considerable opposition from landowners, millers and others, the Bill was passed by Parliament and received the Royal Assent on 7th May, 1793 [33 Geo.III. cap. 102]

The junction of the Derby and Erewash Canals. The canal beyond the bridge has been infilled.

Chapter Four

Construction of the Line

In contrast to certain other canals, which had been started during the previous decade, work on constructing the canal had to wait until after the first formal meeting of the Committee of the Proprietors. This was on 6th July, 1793 at the Bell Inn, Derby and, apart from making a first call of £10 per share on the shareholders, the main business was to confirm the appointment of Benjamin Outram as Engineer to the company.

Work commenced in August, not only in cutting the canal but also on the railway from Little Eaton, using several gangs of men recruited where possible from the locality of the canal, this reduced the need for tents etc., for the work force. The multiple starts meant that work was proceeding so fast that the committee at their October meeting had to make a second call of £10 on the shareholders.

The following month's committee meetings heard that enquiries had been made for the supply of rails for the railway and that Joseph Butler of Chesterfield was able to supply at £10 10s. 0d. (£10.50). The minute reads:

> Resolved that the proposal of Mr Joseph Butler for supplying cast metal rails at £10 10s. per ton to be delivered at Little Eaton in the month of February next be and the same is hereby accepted and that a contract be entered into with him by Mr Upton on behalf of the Company.

Contracts for the work had been let in four sections, and it is apparent from the minutes that 'Lobbying' of committee members by colliery owners together with the need to start and obtain revenue, that the Derby to Little Eaton section of the canal and the railway received special attention.

On 11th May, 1795, the Derby to Little Eaton section of the canal and the railway from Little Eaton to Denby were opened to traffic, some 9 miles [14.5 km] in total, as reported in the *Derby Mercury*:

> ...at about two o'clock the same day, the first boat laden with between 40 and 50 tons of that useful article [coals] arrived in town from the pits at Denby, belonging to William Drury Lowe Esq., of Locko, who generously ordered them to be given to the poor, and on Tuesday they were distributed accordingly.

By the end of the month the Sandiacre line was open and again a boat of coals was sent into Derby, this time by Edward Miller Mundy. On the occasion of the opening of the Sandiacre line, Benjamin Outram stated that the whole undertaking would be completed by Michaelmas, 1796.

Phoenix lock on the Derwent branch in 1905.

The minutes are vague as to the completion of the short section and Phoenix lock, which were the connections to the River Derwent, this section when opened allowed boats to proceed some 1½ miles up stream to the mills at Darley, the limit of navigation on the old Derwent Navigation. It would appear that both these sections were in use before the end of July 1795. ['Walters and Greensmith' were Millers at Darley and Samuel Evans and Co. had a Paper Mill at Darley.]

On the Derby to Swarkestone section, progress was delayed due to a shortage of funds and a further call of £5 per share was made. This allowed work to resume and by February 1796, the weir across the River Derwent had been completed. It was 300 ft [91.5 m] in length and had several uses:

[a] to maintain a constant depth of water to allow navigation
[b] to store water for several mills
[c] to carry a water feed within the weir, this provided a hydraulic connection to the Phoenix lock section and to the Derby to Swarkestone section
[d] to carry a wooden towpath bridge (known as the long bridge.)

Other works required included a cast-iron aqueduct (known as Holmes aqueduct) 40 feet [12 m] in length to carry the canal over Mill Fleam. This was claimed to be a world first, cast by the Outram Company at their works in Butterly, a similar aqueduct was also used on the embankment where the Cuttle Brook was crossed and on the 19th June, 1796 it was reported that the line to the Trent was complete.

CONSTRUCTION OF THE LINE

The total cost was in excess of £100,000, some £90,000 having been raised by calls on the 600 shares issued, the remainder by means of loans and debts.

If we look at the extract from *Bradshaw's Canals and Navigable Rivers for 1904* (*see Appendix Six*), we see that it gives a main line [junction with Erewash Canal to its junction with the Trent and Mersey] of 14 miles 4 furlongs in length, no mention is made of a further length to the River Trent, this is detailed at the end of *Chapter Seven*.

Derby Canal Co. dredger, 1930.
Courtesy of Derby Museums and Art Gallery, Picture the Past.

The murals under the bridge carrying the A514 over the canal, at Shelton lock. They were painted in 1990 by the pupils of Merrill School.

Chapter Five

The Railway or Gangway

The gangway as built consisted of a main line from the wharf at Little Eaton to the pits at Smithy Houses. It was single track with numerous passing places or crossing and remained so until its closure in 1908. As traffic grew, so the number of passing places was increased, and by 1825 there were nine crossing in use instead of the three that were there originally.

The original rails or plates supplied by Joseph Butler of Wingerworth Iron Furnace and Killamarsh Forge were of cast-iron, 3 ft [91 cm] in length of 'L' section, with a 4 in. [10cm] high flange in the centre tapering to 2 in. [5 cm] at the ends. The base was a full 4 in. [10cm] in width throughout with a half-circle cast in the ends. The half-circles when placed next to other formed a hole the rails to the stone blocks, wooden plugs [preferably oak] being inset into the stone blocks; the rail ends then placed over the plug and a wrought-iron spike with a large head was driven into the plug so holding the rail in position. The rails as supplied weighed 28 pounds [12.7 kilos] to the yard [91 cm].

A rail about nine feet in length found in 1991 near Hill Top Farm.

A stone sleeper, with two holes to take wooden plugs for the spikes that held the rails in place.

The stone blocks were of Gritstone, obtained from one of the quarries adjacent to the route of the line at Coxbench and Jack O' Darley's Bridge. The dimensions of the blocks were a nominal 1 ft 6 in. [45 cm] in length and width and 1 ft [30.5 cm] deep. The hole to take the plug was 2½ in. [6cm] in diameter and around 4 to 5 in. [10 to 12.5 cm] deep.

In 1797, a Mr Barnes when laying down a railway at the Lawson Colliery, Newcastle-upon-Tyne used 'stone blocks' and several writers have since claimed that this was the first line to use the stone blocks. However credit must go to Outram as he had constructed the Little Eaton line two years previously and was also working on the Peak Forest Tramway using the same techniques.

In practice this method of holding the rails in position by means of the half-holes cast in the ends was unsatisfactory. If the spikes were not fixed square, the rails were prone to move causing derailments, so later rails were cast with a fixing hole 2 in. [5 cm] from either end, additional holes being drilled in the stone blocks. Where the track was required to cross a road, a trough or 'U' section rail was used; the flanges of which were uniform in height for the length of the rail. On one flange, notches were cast in so as to provide a grip for the wheels of the vehicles crossing the line; this helped vehicles with narrow wheels, as the notches prevented slewing and the vehicle getting stuck in the track. The gauge of the line if measured between the insides of the of the upright flanges was 4 ft 4 in. [132 cm] and if measured over the outside of the flange a fraction over 4 ft 4½ in. [136 cm].

Bertram Baxter in *Stone Blocks and Iron Rails* gives the gauge as 3 ft 6 in. [106 cm], whereas Cyril Hall in *Modern Railway Working* published in 1912 gives the gauge as 4 ft 6 in. [140 cm] between the 'ledges' and this is

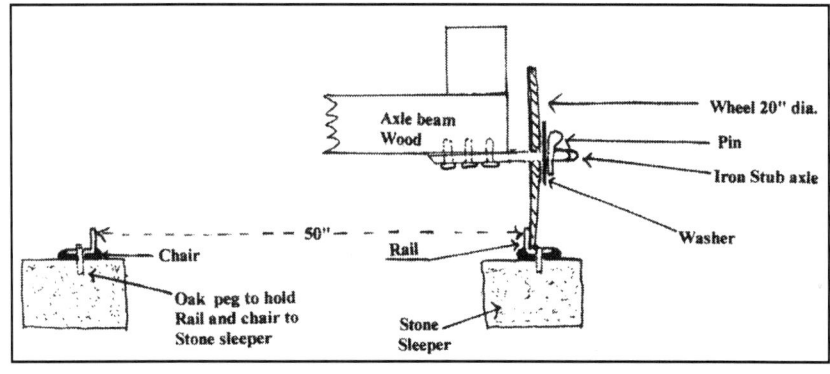

Detail of the track and of the fittings that attached the wheels to the chassis.

substantiated by Mark Fryer in his *History of Denby*. I therefore feel that it is safe to say that the gauge was 4 ft 6 in. [140 cm], as we must remember that the waggons had wheels that 'floated' on their axles and would have ridden on any track laid with a gauge of between 4 ft 5 in. and 4 ft 7 in. [134 to 139 cm]. The pointwork was extremely simple and yet effective; a moving tongue, pivoted at the head was either kicked or levered to face in the desired direction; no point levers or other methods of locking were used, as the pivots were in themselves stiff enough to hold the tongue in place. In addition to two sections with tongues or switch plates, an X-plate with double flanges on the arms, together with the pivoted tongue was the hardware necessary to form a point or turnout.

The line was built as Jessop had suggested with a gradual rise from Little Eaton to Smithy Houses, ascending by over 100 ft [30 metres] in 4½ miles [7.2 km]. Unlike several of the railways and tramways which had Outram as an engineer, either on a consultation basis or as resident engineer, the Little Eaton was not worked on the gravity system, instead teams or gangs of horses were used in both directions, the gradient helping in this case as the major part of the traffic was down from Smithy Houses.

Appendix Two sets out the details of who supplied casting and rails to the Canal Company in its early years.

Pointwork on the approach to the wharf in Little Eaton. The Clock House is on the left and to its right behind the wall is the Midland Railway's goods shed.

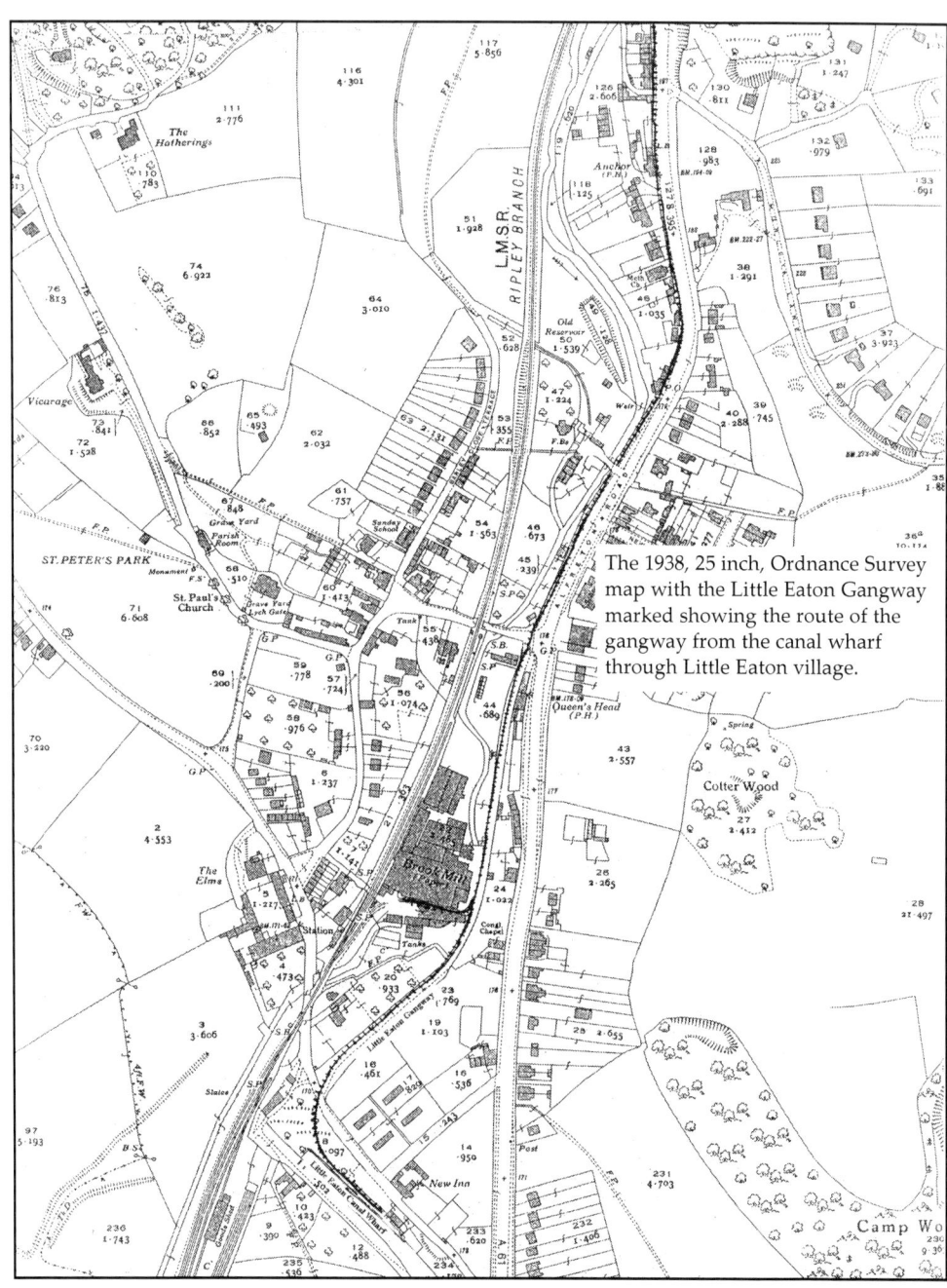

The 1938, 25 inch, Ordnance Survey map with the Little Eaton Gangway marked showing the route of the gangway from the canal wharf through Little Eaton village.

Branches to and from the Main Line

1. At Little Eaton – a spur into the yard of the Brook Paper Mill operated by the canal company.
   [Derby Canal Company's plan of 1870]
2. Near Jack O' Darley's Bridge – a branch to a stone quarry.
   [Mentioned in Minute Book and by Farey in 1817]
3. At Coxbench – to quarry at Horsey.
   [Mentioned in Minute Book, by Farey, not on plan of 1879, but thought to have been in use after this date. A minute of March 1876 states: The Secretary reported that the matter between the Company and Mr Sitwell with reference to the railway over the tramway to the Stone Quarry would pay the Company £100 per year.' Mr Sitwell had for some year's prior been a user of the gangway and was now proposing to establish a connection with the Midland branch to Ripley.]
4. At Lower Kilbourne to Kilbourne Colliery.
   [On plan of 1870]
5. At Kilbourne to Cinder Hill Colliery.
   [On Sanderson's plan of 1835]
6. The Openwoodgate / Belper lines – *see Appendix Four.*
7. Branch from Smithy House to Denby Hall Colliery, north of Salterwood.
   [Priestley (1831) gives a branch ¾ mile to collieries north of Salterwood, shown on Sanderson's plan as a branch to Denby Colliery, Baxter gives this as branch to Denby Hall Colliery, with a sub-branch to Salterwood Colliery, he adds that in 1949 traces were still to be seen. I feel that as fresh pits were sunk and old ones closed the lines were moved around and that at different periods they all existed.]

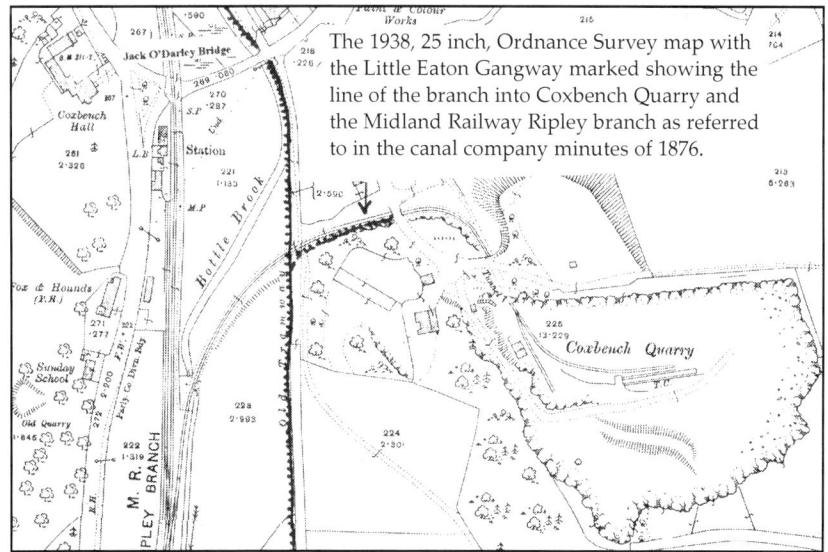

The 1938, 25 inch, Ordnance Survey map with the Little Eaton Gangway marked showing the line of the branch into Coxbench Quarry and the Midland Railway Ripley branch as referred to in the canal company minutes of 1876.

8. Branch from Smithy Houses to Olddenby Colliery (Old Denby Colliery) via Godbers wood.
   [Priestly 1831, Sanderson 1835 also give a branch from Smithy Houses 1½ Miles by the potteries to extensive coal workings near Denby Hall.]
9. Branch to Robey West Colliery (Parish of Denby).
   [Farey gives as 6 miles from Little Eaton and ⅝ths mile from Denby Hall. An unnamed line is shown by Sanderson, which appears to agree with Farey.]
10. Branch from Smithy Houses via the College and Denby Pottery to Marehay.
    [A realignment of 8 above.]

Traffic

19th century traffic carried by tramway and canal was summarized by the late Arthur Guest in 1968, using canal toll books, colliery records and newspaper articles, his list amended by subsequent research:

Goods out

1. Coal – the prime use.
2. Pottery from Belper and Denby – stored in crate shed at canal head.
3. Paper from two mills in Little Eaton.
4. Scythe Stones and Grind Stones from the Morley Moor quarries.
5. Dressed stone from the Little Eaton and Coxbench quarries.
6. Glazed pipes, house bricks from kilns at Denby and Horsley.
7. Paint and Colour from Coxbench Colour works for delivery to Messrs Leach Neale & Co. of Spondon.
8. The finished products of Little Eaton Bleach Mills.

Goods inward included

1. Gypsum and rags for the paper mills.
2. Road Stone.
3. 'Night Soil' from Derby.
4. Agricultural feed stuffs. A considerable amount of animal feeds came from the Gainsborough area, travelling by canals all the way to Little Eaton.
5. Timber.

It is interesting to look at the local trades in the Bottle Valley that provided traffic for the Little Eaton line, even the geology of the area is important. At Horsley Woodhouse the stone is a Wingerfield Flagstone outcrop much used in and around Derby for kerbs and paving, whereas at Coxbench fine grained grit makes first class building stone.

In 1800 coal provided 70 per cent of the revenue for the canal and

THE RAILWAY OR GANGWAY

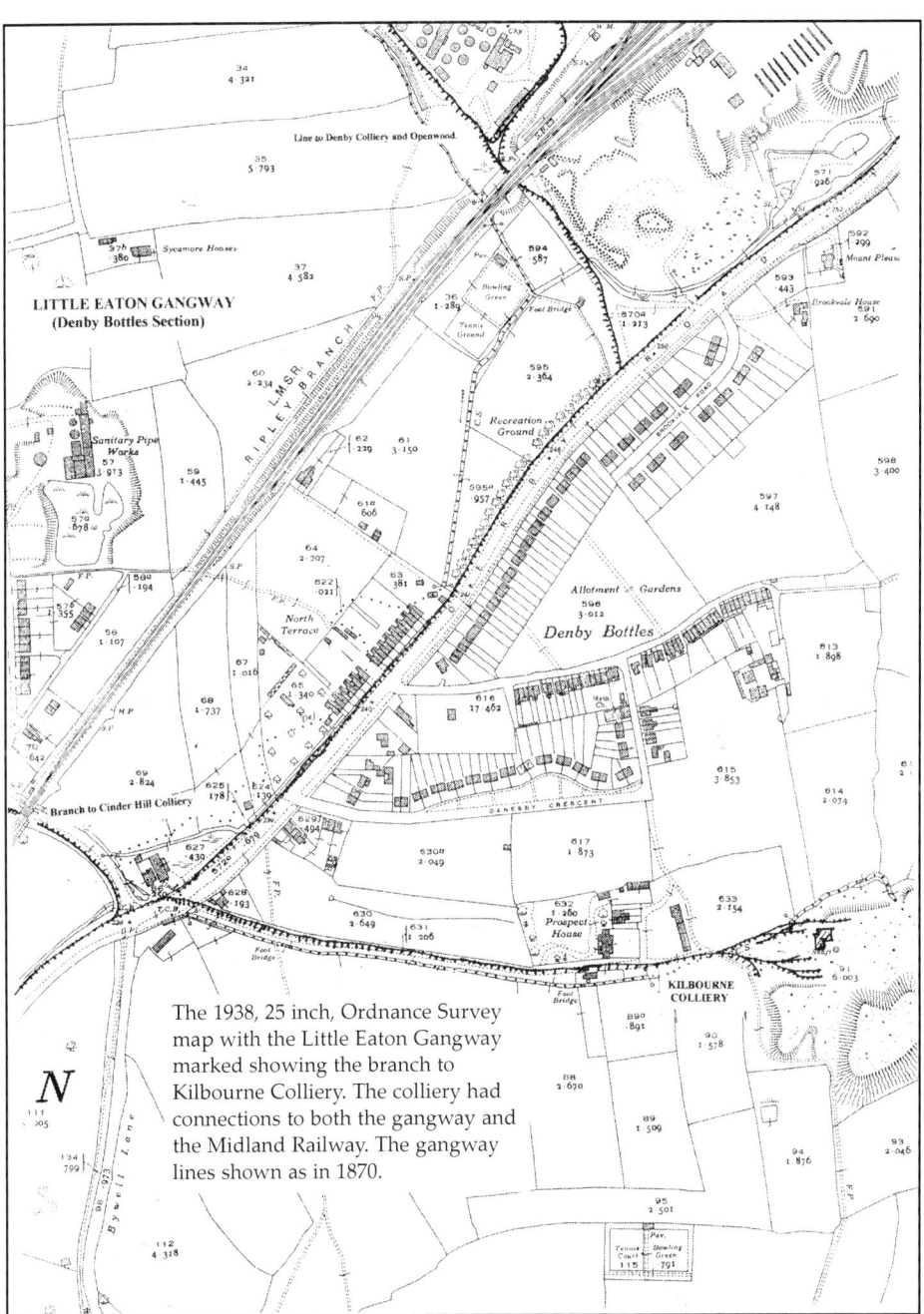

The 1938, 25 inch, Ordnance Survey map with the Little Eaton Gangway marked showing the branch to Kilbourne Colliery. The colliery had connections to both the gangway and the Midland Railway. The gangway lines shown as in 1870.

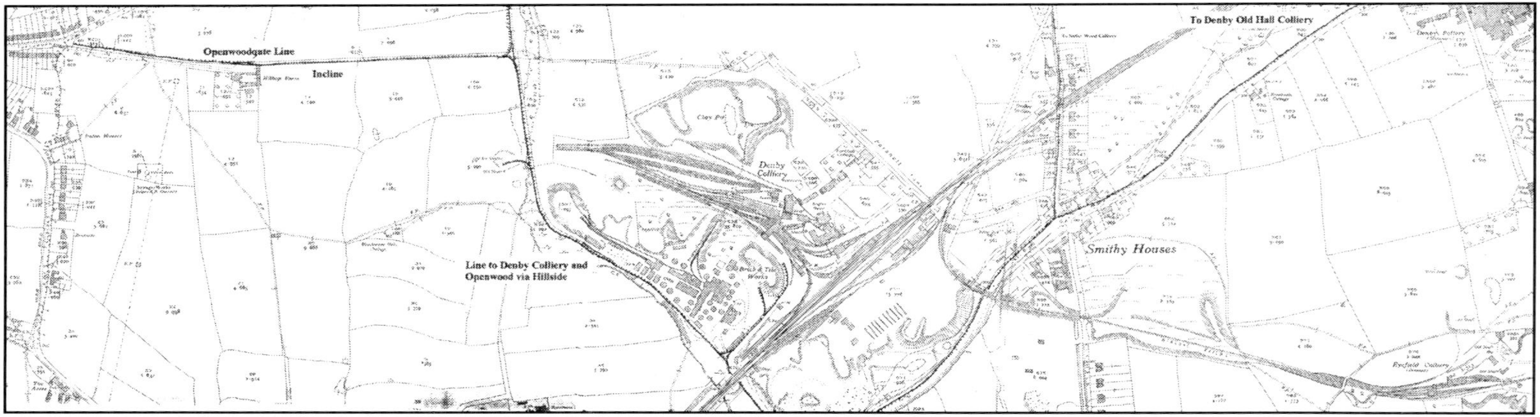

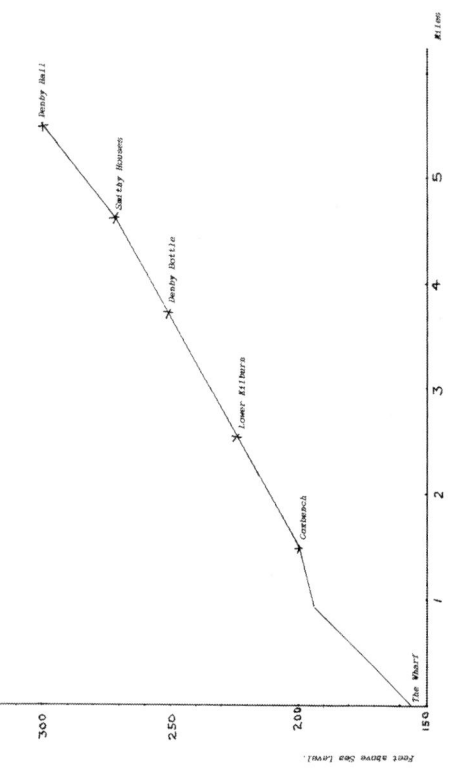

The 1938, 25 inch, Ordnance Survey map with the Little Eaton Gangway marked showing the lines to Openwoodgate (*left*), and Smithy Houses (*right*).

Gradient Profile of the Little Eaton Gangway. If the canal had carried on to Smithy Houses it would have needed seven locks with a rise of 20 feet each. In addition it would have needed a large reservoir to ensure water for the canal.

Denby coals comprised 50 per cent of the total coal traffic. Denby Pottery first used the gangway for crated stone ware bottles in 1820, but thefts from unattended waggons combined with high breakage levels and even higher freight charges, forced the Pottery owner Joseph Bourne to seek alternative methods of shipment. This was partly solved by designating one of the sheds on the wharf, a crate store with secure locks.

In the early 1800s when traffic was at its peak, it is recorded that as many of 27 boats were at Little Eaton wharf on the same day.
(*See also Appendix Three.*)

View of the derelict trackbed north of Coxbench, May 1947.
H. Murray / A. Rimmer Collection

Chassis and waggons at Little Eaton wharf c.1920. In the background on the right is the signal box of the Midland Railway line from Derby to Ripley.
Derby Local Studies Library

Pair of waggons stored for preservation, May 1947.
H. Murray / A. Rimmer Collection

Chapter Six

Rolling Stock

The waggons used on the railway or gangway, as it became known locally, were in many ways very advanced in their design. A waggon consisted of two sections, an undercarriage or chassis and a body or box.

The undercarriage was constructed of timber with cast-iron fittings and wheels; the timbers were in the main of square section, held together with hand-forged bolts, with the main timbers being fashioned from 6 in. [15 cm] square oak; similar timbers supported the stub axles, and also acted as dumb buffer beams. Four cast-iron wheels (later replacements were of wrought-iron) some 2 ft 4 in. [71 cm] in diameter, with a tread thickness of 1½ in. [4 cm] ran on cast stub axles. A large iron washer and a flat cotter pin secured the wheel to the axle. The wheels ran on the outside of the upright rail flanges and they floated on the axles. This floating allowed the chassis to accept deviations in the track gauge as occurred at 'turn-outs' or where the line curved. The wheels were brittle, breakages occurred fairly frequently, so spare wheels were placed at intervals alongside the route. The undercarriage or tram as it was called by the gangers weighed in the region of 10 cwt [500 kilo].

At least three types of body were used, the principal type for coal traffic were 5 ft 9 in. [175 cm] in length, 3 ft 7½ in. [110 cm] wide and 2ft [61 cm] deep with a 'top-board' adding a further 1 ft 5 in. [43 cm] to the

Detail of a waggon from Denby Colliery, showing the pin and washer used to hold the wheel to the axle. This was the type of waggon used on the line from the 1790s to its closure.

A waggon on the gangway, the chains on its body allow the box to be lifted from the chassis and loaded on to a barge. Detachable top boards have been fitted to the sides of the waggon to increase its carrying capacity. *Derby Local Studies Library*

A waggon from Denby Colliery on display at Chaterley Whitfield Colliery Museum in 1990.

depth; this type of body would carry between 45 & 48 cwt [2275 & 2400 kilos] of lump coal. One end of the body was open to allow the lump coal to be stacked and it was retained by a series of chains fitted with tensioning levers. One of the reasons for stacking the coal by hand was that there was little if any sale for slack coal in the 18th and early 19th centuries, Most of the tips that existed contained a large percentage of small pieces and coal dust. In recent years this small or slack coal has been recovered, mainly for use in power stations, then the remaining heaps have been landscaped or used to in fill the areas where subsidence had occurred.

The second type of body used mainly for stone was similar to that used for coal in size, it had slatted sides and no top boards. For mixed traffic, a smaller body known as a 'mule' was introduced; designed to carry around one ton [1000 kilos] they were used to carry corn and provisions up the line from Little Eaton. Where a farm was fairly close to the line, the carters who used this type of body would run the waggons off the line and haul the waggon to its destination. This practice was frowned on by the canal authorities for two reasons, damage to the rails and it caused delays; a mention is made in the minutes of instructions given to carters to cease such practices.

Motive power as previously mentioned was by horses, references to the use of oxen have occurred in articles which appeared in the local press over the years. The only item the author has found which even remotely substantiates this idea, was when Edward Thompson Limited, Civil Engineers of Derby, were laying a 24 in. [60 cm] water main along the Duffield Road in Little Eaton. This was in the spring of 1952, they unearthed several lengths of the old gangway track where it crossed the road, and adjacent was found the odd ox-shoe. There is certainly no mention of oxen in the canal co.'s minute book, however it may be that one of the private carters used oxen.

When the waggons of coal or stone were loaded, they were made up into gangs (hence the local name of gangway), and a team of horses would then take them down the railway to the wharf at Little Eaton. Here a crane was situated to lift the laden bodies off the undercarriages and place them into a boat for onward carriage, in the main this system was used for supplies to the Derby wharves where similar cranes were installed. Where the coal was to travel any distance by boat, the container was lifted on to the boat, the lifting slings on the gate end and the retaining chains undone, slowly the container would be raised and the load of coal would be transferred to the boat with if the crane operator was careful, little breakage of the coal.

Detail of the brackets that held the detachable box on the waggon chassis.

This system of detachable bodies as adopted by Outram, was based on one that was already in use on the Lings Colliery line (north of Wingfield Town) devised by Joseph Butler around 1775. According to contemporary reports, waggons ran on a plateway from pits at Lings to the village of Ankerbold, the body then being transferred to a horse-drawn road vehicle to a wharf on the Chesterfield Canal. Here the body was transferred to a boat for the journey to Killamarsh wharf where the process was reversed and the body once more conveyed to Mr Butler's iron forge. The length of this line is given as 1.275 miles [2,200 metres], it has been a matter of conjecture as to why the line did not carry on to the canal and save one transhipment. Recent research into the land ownership between the end of Mr Butler's land and the canal has shown that he was unable to obtain wayleaves over the Ankerbold to canal section, partly as it would have had to go close to a large house owned by local gentry. The cost of obtaining Parliamentary Powers for such a short section would have been prohibitive.

The use of detachable bodies on the tram and plateways of Derbyshire are some of the earliest uses on record and are the 'grandparents' of the container system that are now used worldwide.

William Jessop had, as we saw in his report, envisaged one horse drawing two waggons, however it was found to be more practical and economical for a team of horses to be coupled to a gang of waggons. This not only made savings in the number of drivers required, but also avoided long waits which occurred at the passing places when single horse teams were used, thus avoiding the expense that would be incurred in making the line double track.

At Little Eaton and indeed at the various wharves on the canal, the cranes which were used to transfer the containers from chassis to boat were provided with four arm chain slings, the hooks on the ends of the arms being placed into eyes on the top corners of the waggon body. Provided the chains were not twisted the body was kept level, allowing the boatman to position the container in the boat. As mentioned previously, coal going further afield was tipped into the boat, for this purpose a set of chains with two quick release catches was used.

In the series of photographs that were taken by a Derby photographer for Mark Fryer shortly before the line closed, gangs of eight waggons hauled by four horses in single file are featured with a 'gang leader' at the head of the leading horse. Where a single horse with one or two waggons were used, mainly on non-coal / stone traffic, the man appears to have been termed 'a carter'. From the canal records it would seem that many of the 'carters' were not employed by the company but by forwarding agents.

Gang of horses, on the site of what is now the Coxbench Bypass, showing the method of harnessing them to the waggons, *circa* 1908.

The harness consisted of a collar from which two broad straps ran along the horse's back and joined under its tail. From these straps two sets of transverse straps hung, one on either side of the horse and loosely connected by a belly chain, the other set placed just forward of the tail supported the spacer bar. The haulage straps ran from the collar, passing through loops on the forward transverse straps and terminating on the wooden spacer bar. Horse to horse or horse to waggon attachment was by chains from the ends of the spacer bars to either side of the following horse's collar or to rings on the waggons. Rings were provided on the underframes for use when moving empties and approximately 1 foot [30cm] above the chassis when hauling loaded waggons, this higher position being more effective and easing the strain on the horse. At Little Eaton wharf a single horse was kept for shunting waggons, in particular empty ones and forming them into gangs for the next ganger with horses to take back up the line. In later years it became custom to use older horses for this work.

A recently located photograph showing two local boats at Little Eaton wharf shows the 'shunting horse' in front of the Clock House and several empty chassis in the foreground.

The last gang of four horses and waggons left Smithy Houses in July 1908, the ganger being a William Wooley. This ended 105 years of horse haulage on the Little Eaton Gangway. A few of the horses worked on for a few years with the canal maintenance teams, they were very useful when clearing weeds or rubbish from the canal and on at least two occasions for ice breaking.

Side view of a gang of horses and loaded waggons.

Chapter Seven

The Route

The Sandiacre Section

The line from its junction with the Erewash Canal at Sandiacre to where it joined the Little Eaton line at Derby was 8 miles and 6 furlongs [14 km] in length with four locks; that raised the canal by 29 ft [8.8 m].

Leaving the Erewash Canal at a point some 3 miles 2 furlongs [5.25 km] from Trent lock and Toll Office, the Derby Canal passed under a road bridge then climbed up two locks to the 136 ft [41 m] contour which it followed for nearly 4 miles [6.4 km] to Coffee Joe Bridge. Here the ground fell away and banks were constructed to retain the canal until it reached the next locks at Borrowash. As the ground was undulating it was necessary to again build embankments, first on one side then on the other until near Spondon embankments were required on either side, these continuing until it reached the junction with the Little Eaton branch.

In 1839 the canal was re-routed for 800 yards [730 m] to allow the construction of the Midland Counties Railway, which was to connect Derby and Nottingham. The railway contractor was to pay a penalty for

Road bridge on Lock Lane, Sandiacre, at the start of the Derby Canal. Immediately beyond this bridge was Sandiacre bottom lock.

Looking along the line of the canal from the bridge on Lock Lane. The chamber of the lock is completely filled so that the footpath along the canal is level with the road over the bridge.

The Navigation Inn at Breaston. The canal has been filled in and picnic tables rest where once boats were tied up while their crews partook of refreshments.

stopping navigation on the canal [£2 per hour]. However the canal company had to stop navigation for emergency repairs and the railway contractor increased his workforce by over 200 men, by so doing he succeeded in completing the railway and canal diversion before the canal was reopened for navigation, at about this time the Top Lock Cottage was built. The railway near this point is in a deep cutting with very strong walls as it lies between the canal and the river. The site of the top lock was lost, but recent trial excavations have located it and strong steel posts now mark the corners,

Near the bottom lock at Borrowash [known also as Shacklecross Lock] an arm was constructed to serve a cotton mill, *Pigot's directory* for 1835 states:

> Upwards of 450 of the inhabitants are employed in the extensive lace-thread Mills of Messrs. Towle and many others in the manufacture of twist thread.

Later the mills under John Towle and Co. were classified as cotton doublers and they also had a Cotton and Lace Mill at Draycott. It is interesting that both mills were on canals. The mill known originally as Borrowash Mill then Shacklecross Mill was demolished in 1993, the site is now a very well set out housing estate, the road names recall the old mill and the canal.

Borrowash Bottom lock excavated in 1998. The lock and its chamber was found to be fairly sound and it was left unearthed. It became overgrown but was cleared again in 2018. At that time the coping stonework, which had been bulldozed into the lock when the canal was closed, was restored to the brick walls.

Most of this section was filled in during the late 1960s, since when both a section of the M1 motorway and a dual carriageway have crossed over its bones. Following an exercize by the Derby Corporation, several lengths were made into a linear footpath, which has provided relaxation and exercise for the local populace. One drawback was that the canal had served as a drain for the surrounding land and since it was filled in, the land either side has become waterlogged in periods of heavy rain. The lock chambers were left in place although filled in and were reminders of the canal. As you walk the route it is interesting to note that many of the public houses took their names from the close proximity of the canal; the Bridge Inn near Sandiacre, the Navigation at Breaston and the Angler's Arms near Spondon. Will we ever see boats tied up alongside any of them whilst their crews partake of the hostel's refreshments?

The Little Eaton Branch

This short section of the canal, 3 miles 1 furlong [5km] in length was the most important section for many years as it linked the main line with the Little Eaton Gangway, as the gangway originally provided the bulk of the traffic, i.e. coal and stone. It ran almost due north on the wast side of the racecourse with four locks, Pasture, Depot, Sharon and Eaton Top.

The Eaton Top lock of the Little Eaton branch in 1905.

Water for this section was in part from the Bottle Brook but a main source was a feeder from the Dam Brook near Breadsall, remains of which were still *in situ* in the early 1980s. An account of the transactions between the canal company and a Mr Thomas Tempest exist. These concern the erection of a weir at a place called Peckwash Mill and the formation of a culvert to supply the Little Eaton line of the canal with water. The wharf at Little Eaton required frequent attention to its fabric, due no doubt to the amount of traffic it handled. Its importance can be gauged in that it had an Agent to manage the wharf and collect tolls. The canal co. minute for 12th February, 1821 in a brief entry states: 'Agent at Little Eaton - Leonard Lead dead, appointed William Wall as Collector of Tolls and Agent.'

Litton Eaton to Smithy Houses

The Act provided for a railway from Little Eaton to Smithy Houses instead of a canal, with clauses that made provision for railways to be built from the main line to collieries, quarries and iron works within 2,000 yds [1,828m.] of the main line.

As built the main line ran from the Little Eaton wharf along the Bottle Brook Valley for 6 miles [9.6 km] to Roby West Common Colliery at Denby with a branch to Denby Hall Colliery. As the coal field was developed other branches were constructed, also local quarries, brickworks and other industries made use of the improved transport afforded by the railway and canal.

Farey gives the following description of the line:

> ...Little Eaton to Bottle Vale, six miles further to Roby West Field Colliery; from this railway extension there is a branch ⅜ mile to Denby Hall Colliery, one was provided for in the Act, East to Smalley Mills and to Horsey Colliery; and there are two small branches into Little Eaton Common Quarries.

Sanderson's map of 1835 shows the railway running from Little Eaton Wharf, past the quarries (no branch being shown) through Horsley Park, Horsley and Kilbourne, a branch running west to a colliery at Cinder Hill, a further branch to an unnamed Colliery and a brick works near Park Hall. At Smithy Houses, the line divided, one line going north via High Park to Denby Colliery, then bearing northeast via Golbers Wood to Old Denby Colliery and an old pit at Godbers Lunn. The other line from Smithy Houses ran via the College and Denby Pottery to Marehay. Several of these lines were built by the

The crane on Little Eaton wharf. There are a couple of boats in the basin, behind them is the Clock House which served as the Wharf Agent's office. The building still stands but is lost in a small industrial estate behind the units that are built on the infilled basin.

colliery owners, from the minute book in would appear that the canal company worked them.

Around 1870, the estate agents that acted for the Derby Canal Company obtained a set of the newly published 25 inch to the mile Ordnance Survey maps and marked on them the boundaries of the land still owned by the canal company, they clearly show the lines as then existing.

The railway left the Little Eaton wharf and almost immediately turned through 90 degrees to the north-east then turned again towards the north-north-west. Here a spur led into Brook Mill (a paper mill for over a century), traces of this section were still visible in 1970. Then through the village following Bottle Brook until it reached the Alfreton Turnpike road, passing under it by Jack O' Darley's Bridge on to Coxbench and Kilburn still running alongside the brook. Then a branch to Kilbourne Colliery with its fairly comprehensive sidings and another to Hill Top Farm with several short spurs to pits, winding engines and brick yards that flourished in the mid-19th century.

The Clock House and a gang of horses with a train of coal.

Looking along the route of the gangway in 1970. The Clock House is in the background to the left of centre.

Jack O' Darley's Bridge with the lines still in place.
Derby Local Studies Library

The remains of the line from Salterwood to Smithy Houses. A few weeks after this photograph was taken, in 1989, the site was cleared so that opencast mine workings could be extended.

Track still in place alongside the Little Eaton to Milford road, *circa* 1930.
Derby Local Studies Library

Trucks in various states of disrepair and piles of lines in Denby Colliery yard.
Derby Local Studies Library

The map then shows the line as owned by the canal company terminating at Smithy Houses. Baxter in *Stone Blocks and Iron Rails* gives the route as shown on the company's map together with a branch south from Godbers Lunn, south to Salterwood and Denby Pottery. The line effectively closed in 1906.

Eric Potter writing in the Butterley Colliery magazine in the 1960s, states that there was almost certainly a branch to the quarries at Coxbench, a branch to Denby Ironworks with others to Basset Pit and Openwoodgate, At the time of writing the article, Mr Potter mentions that several slag heaps had been removed near Denby, exposing an old embankment near to the road.

Today the remains of the railway are hard to find. In the 1980s the wharf was home to a small industrial estate, with the old Clock House partly hidden behind other buildings. Where the gangway left the wharf, lorries exit a road haulier's yard, then you pass the site of the old paper mill, now another industrial complex. For the next 100 metres or so, the route is easy to follow. It passes behind the 'Queen's Head Inn' [or so locals say it's front, for the Inn appears to have been remodelled and turned round when the former A61 road (now the B6179) was an important route up the valley], then by the green to Jack O'Darleys Bridge. One may still go through the bridge, it is well worth a visit to see how well the stones were tooled or dressed in a 'herring bone pattern', all the stones fit neatly together and if you look hard you can find an odd mason's mark.

After the bridge the route fades away, most lost under 'road improvements', gone are the stone watering troughs which were an indication to the location of the passing places, one survived near Kilbourne until the late 1960s. No traces remain of the line beyond this point, considerable development having taken place since the closure of the pits and subsequent land reclamation.

The Derby to Swarkeston Section

From the junction with the Little Eaton branch the canal continued towards Derby, meeting the branch to the upper section of the Derwent River followed by White Bear lock, here it fell to meet the River Derwent, the entrance to which was controlled by Peggs Flood lock. Across the River, Day's lock lifted the canal to Gandy's wharf followed by the Gas Works, built close to the canal so that supplies of coal could be readily and even more important, cheaply transported.

Fishing in the Derby Canal near Erasmus Street, Derby around 1930.
Courtesy Mrs Bishop

48　　　THE LITTLE EATON GANGWAY AND DERBY CANAL

Long Bridge and the weir on the River Derwent in 1905.

Locks at Siddals Road. *Derby Local Studies Library*

The canal's stone edging still in place along the route of the canal between Sinfin Moor Lane and Shelton lock.

The junction between the Derby and Trent and Mersey Canals at Swarkestone.

Most of the canal in Derby has vanished under the Derby Inner Ring Road complex.

After Alvaston came the two locks at Shelton, falling 12 feet[3.5 m], then across Sinfin Moor to its junction with the Trent and Mersey Canal at Swarkestone. By the 1950s this section had become overgrown and after the official closure of the canal parts were filled in. However you could still trace it from near to Wilmorton Tertiary College to Swarkestone, most of the route incorporates a section of the Little Eaton to Melbourne Cycleway.

The last surviving Toll House on the Derby Canal is now the clubhouse for the Swarkestone Boat Club.

River Derwent Branch.

A short section of canal was built to allow boats to bypass a weir and gain access to the section of river above the Silk Mill Weir. It was only 2 furlongs [800m] in length and had one lock. The River Derwent was at one time navigable for about a mile [1.6km] from the Silk Mill up to the mills at Darley Abbey, where the weir providing power for Evan's Boar Head Mill, prevented passage further upstream.

The Swarkestone to River Trent Section

As mentioned in *Chapter Four*, this section was built but was out of use within a few years, no traces remain. It is shown on Outram's Survey map of 1792 as requiring one lock at the northern end approx. 400 metres above the Trent and Mersey lock at Swarkestone. It is believed to have needed an additional lock at the river end but I have not been able to substantiate this as all the maps for the early part of the 19th century are not clear on this point. Papers lodged with the minute books show that this short section [3 furlongs] with its locks was a loss-maker. This was due to lock keeper's wages, high maintenance costs, due in part to having a river at its southern end which was liable to floods etc. which washed away or silted up the junction. Couple this with the compensation toll of 1s. [5p] paid to the Trent and Mersey authorities, the abandonment of the idea to bring a canal from Cloud Hill to join the canal, then when labour shortages occurred during the Napoleonic wars and rising prices, the Derby Canal Committee allowed this short section to decay, it is highly doubtful if any traffic was carried after 1818.

Chapter Eight

Administration of the Company

The day to day running of the canal company was in the hands of the Company Secretary and the Resident Engineer, but their powers were very limited, any major matters having to wait for the next meeting of the committee. This body had powers not unlike those exercised today by the Board of Directors of a public company.

At the meeting held at the 'Kings Head Inn' on 22nd February, 1796, it was recorded: 'Some of the members of the Committee having attended this morning at the Bason at Little Eaton to examine the state of the Wharves and works there...' As a result of the report submitted it was agreed that the -

> Railway west of the Bason should be extended 20 yards [18 metres] further to the South and that another Railway should be laid parallel at a convenient distance west ward thereof for the greater convenience of unloading the coal and that the wharf should be extended westward into Mr Friguall's Close, to a line of stakes put down there this morning and that the road on the east side of the Bason between the Toll house and bridge ought to be laid to the Wharf and a new road made parallel thereto out of the west end of a piece of Land belonging to Mr Brooks.

Later the same year following a visit to the wharf, the committee ordered 'A new crane for the Old Wharf to lift from 16 to 20 hundredweight and another for 30 to 40 hundredweight. [This is surprising as the waggons weighed empty 2 cwt and coals up to 45 cwt.]

On the 24th April, 1797 the meeting was held at the Bell Inn, and complaints voiced, 'The Coal waggons frequently pop off the railway at the passing or crossing places.' On the recommendations of the Engineer, 'substitute rails of so much tops (weight) were to be used.'

Other complaints led to a series of By Laws being made and at a meeting, held this time at the George Inn during December 1803, various rules relating to the railway were issued.

It had become general practice for the committee to inspect the various lines of the canal and railway on an annual basis, the committee appointing various members together with an engineer to inspect a line and then for a report to be submitted on the actions taken or proposed. In the report of 30th May, 1821, Messrs Tudor and Challeston's report for the 'Sandyacre' line mentioned:

> a. Mr Clarke encroached on the canal with a stable lately built.
> b. The rope walk on the towing path side should be taken away or altered to prevent any complaints from Messrs Mellor and Co.

A platelayer standing by a section of track of inverted fish-belly pattern rails similar to those laid in the 1790s. This view clearly shows the stone block sleepers and the raised walkway for horses.

A gang of horses on the Little Eaton to wharf section with coal waggons.

c. The lock at James Dawsons wants some repairs also the Lock near to Sandyacre.
d. The Wood Bridges want cleaning, painting and repairing.
e. New House at Draycott Bridge encroaches on the towing path.
f. The gate and post is gone from the towing path at the footbridge.
g. The cut to Mr Wottens late Dock should be made up, the dock now part of a garden.
h. Brick Bridges on the canal to be pointed and repaired, to be coloured with Barrow lime wash and numbered.
i. The Towing Path wants a few repairs.

As a result of this report we find at the December meeting it was agreed that a Mr Joseph Mooley, who had erected the new house at Draycott Bridge was to pay 18 shillings for the purchase of 9 square yards of land.

Messrs Jessop and Braugham had 'perambulated' the Swarkestone line and their report included:

a. The towing path near the first lock is too high and should be lowered.
b. Osmaston occupation Bridge leading into the meadows in front of the Hall wants repairing, the wood is decayed where it joins the stone work.
c. The balance beam is bad.
d. Bank on Swinfin Moor on the towing path side wants raising in several places.
e. The culvert under the canal on the Moor wants pointing.
f. The Bridges to be repaired coloured with lime wash and renumbered.

In 1824 the Little Eaton Line and Railway were inspected by Messrs Chatterton, Tudor and Saudows and their report makes mention of:

a New wharf at Little Eaton wants Breast Wall of good large stones.
b Second lock up from Derby, Beam is broken.
c Towing path between Breadsall Bridge and Eaton wants repairing.
d Railway near Bason at Eaton wants raising and re-laying, same near Bleach Works and Smithy Houses.
e. The Railway at Eaton should be lengthened to the end of Walls House to give room for a stock of coal.
f. The top end of the wharf is occupied by Stone Bottle Crates.

A number of the committee members met at Smithy Houses on Saturday 29th October, 1827, with several colliery owners and their agents regarding a proposed extension to the colliery of Mr Streetly. After discussing the situation, a special meeting was called to approve the expenditure of £1,571 for a railway line to the colliery.

Messrs Harris, Davenport and Co. were appointed contractors to build the extension and Mr Streetly was to act as guarantor. The railway extension cost more than the estimate and the committee, after a series of site meetings with the contractors, agreed to settle for £1,700 12s. 3d.

Steam traction for railways was a fact by 1830, costs of transhipping coals at Little Eaton were rising and the improved turnpike road built by the Alfreton Road Trustees was allowing carter's to buy their coals at the pits, carry it along the new highway and sell it in Derby at a lower price than that shipped via the canal, this despite several reductions in the canal rates...

On 2nd November, the Committee resolved:

> That the expediency of making a New Railway from Smithy Houses to Little Chester on the most approved principles with a view to the conveyance of coals and other articles by means of Locomotive engines moved by Steam and of applying to Parliament for an Act to authorise the continuation of such a railway from Little Eaton to Derby along the line of the canal and to discontinue the canal be taken into serious considerations of the committee.
>
> That Mr Stephenson, an eminent Engineer, be employed to survey the proposed line and estimate the expense of making Rail Roads and to estimate the expense per ton mile at which goods may be conveyed along the new railways.

George Stephenson accepted the commission and lost no time in making the survey; at the committee meeting held on the 15th February, 1831 a letter from Stephenson was read:

> Derby, Sunday Morning
>
> Dear Sir,
> I enclose you my report upon the Little Eaton Branch of the Derby Canal and in case the committee should wish a survey of the valley up which the Canal and Railways runs, the Surveyor should be instructed to make a survey of the ground lying between the River Derwent and the Canal, and to include the whole of the low land on each side of the Brook by the side of which the Railway runs.
> I am Dr. Sir Yours truly
> Geo. Stephenson.

(The report is included as *Appendix Five*)

The project was deferred from meeting to meeting and shelved when the trade from the collieries increased in 1832, a very short-sighted policy in view of subsequent developments.

At the April 1832 committee meeting, an application was received from Mr Holden for an additional railway at Little Eaton. A site meeting was arranged for the following Monday and as a result it was ordered:

> ....that an additional Branch of Railway be made at Eaton for the accommodation of Mr Holden, the estimate of the expense of which is below.

Cast iron rails - 40½ at £8 per ton	£16	4s. 0d.
Blocks – 108 at 4½ each	£2	0s. 6d.
Nails 6s. 99d., Workmanship £1.15s. 0d.	£2	1s. 9d.
	£20	6s. 3d.

The additional lines were provided as well as a weighing machine at Coxbench, mainly for the weighing of coal traffic.

Later the same year the company was offered the railway to Colley's Colliery for £700. This railway known as Bulmers Railway was inspected by the company's Agent; when his report was to hand the company decided for the present to defer the purchase as 'Mr Colley's Colliery was not at work'.

The wharf at Little Eaton, where a load of coal has just been drawn by a gang of horses. The chimney of the Brook Paper Mill smokes in the background.

Amongst other duties the committee was also responsible for the appointment of staff and a typical entry is on 30th March, 1841: 'Appointed George Rickard to be Agent and Bookkeeper at a Salary of £80 per year.' This appointment was to fill the vacancy, which occurred when the previous Agent, Mr Grime, left to fill the vacancy which occurred as Agent for Sir George Crewes. Mr Grime had been appointed in November 1833 at a salary of £60 per annum.

Fixing of rates and allowing drawbacks (rebates) was another duty with which the committee was constantly concerned. The canal had been built at the end of the 'Canal Mania' and might be termed a second-generation canal: as such it suffered competition from established ones such as the Erewash, Cromford and Trent and Mersey. Rates were a problem; as early as 1797 drawbacks were being considered for coal and building stone traffics, and the rate for limestone conveyed from Swarkestone to Little Eaton for transhipment was reduced to 3d. a ton. In the following year a special rate was introduced for traffic carried down the line from Denby to Little Eaton of 1s. 5d. per ton, with free carriage from Little Eaton to Derby. This lasted until 1811, was re-introduced in 1815 and continued until 1820.

In March 1824, a Mr Lowe, owner of the New Delph Colliery at Denby asked the clerk if the company would reduce the rate on coal travelling down the railway to Little Eaton and thence to Derby as 'the sale of his New Delph and soft coals had been lately much reduced', the committee considered his request and it is recorded that:

> Considering the large quantity of coals that come from Denby by land carriage and being anxious to increase the sales of Denby coals conveyed on the Eaton line and railway. It was resolved that in this case, Mr Lowe would reduce his price of the New Delph and Soft Coals by ten pence per ton and engage not to allow any reduction of price to land carriers buying at the pits; the committee would allow a reduction of 5d. per ton, it being considered that no less a reduction in the price of coals would allow it a ready sale.

In November, 1828, Messrs Harris, Davenport and Co. were allowed a reduction of 5d. per ton on coals shipped from Denby Old Colliery to the Grand Trunk Canal, providing that they shipped at least 100 tons per month. Drawbacks were also allowed to various quarry owners who shipped stone from the Coxbench Quarries to the Midland and London areas. This traffic during the 1820s was very heavy, as a consequence the passing places between the wharf at Little Eaton were increased from three to six.

Chapter Nine

Closure

The closure of the canal occurred in phases; as mentioned previously the short section from Swarkestone to the River Trent was out of use by 1820 and abandoned shortly afterwards. Traffic on the Little Eaton line was hit by the opening of the Derby to Ripley branch of the Midland Railway in 1856. After that date the traffic on this line decreased to such an extent that in 1897, the Clerk to the Derby Canal entered into correspondence with the Board of Trade under the provisions of the Railway and Canal Traffic Act of 1888 to seek an order to abandon the line. In a reply from the Board of Trade dated 1898, he was advised that Board of Trade [Railways Department] did not feel that Section 45 of the Act applied and a Bill before Parliament would be necessary

No further action seems to have occurred until 1909, when a letter to the Board of Trade enquired if the Act now applied as the line had been disused for about 12 months, still the answer was 'No' [the last waggons left Smithy Houses in July 1908 for Little Eaton, the gang driver was a William Wooley].

On the 3rd August, 1911 a further letter was sent stating that the line had been out of use for three years, this time the Board of Trade in a letter dated 9th August replied in the affirmative. The formal application was prepared and submitted. On the 28th December, the Board of Trade said it would now consider the application, but first the Canal Company must serve notice on all the adjoining landowners and any one else who may be affected by the proposed closure, including local authorities. In addition it would be necessary to publish the proposed closure in at least two local papers for two week.

The then Clerk, C .K. Eddowes, carried out the instructions and in the main, the replies from local landowners were in the nature of requests to purchase the portions of land that adjoined their lands. Approval was given for the abandonment subject to the approval of the shareholders.

The sale of the land to local authorities and landowners was delayed, in part by the First World War, the final sales being completed in the 1920s. The section from Jack O' Darley's Bridge to Tad Lane was sold to the Trustees of the will of the late Sir John H. Crewe. The section from Kilburn Toll Bar to Smithy Houses to Capt. J.A.E. Drury-Lowe; the section from Belper / Kilburn cross roads along the side of the main road as far as the boundary stone by the school at Smithy Houses was sold to another member of the Lowe family. It is interesting to note that the families who over a century previously had been foremost in promoting the canal still had interests as landowners in the area.

Canal warehouse on Bridgewater Wharf, the Cockpit, Derby.
Courtesy of Derby Museums and Art Gallery, Picture the Past

Shortly afterwards most of the traffic on the canal section from Derby to Little Eaton ceased, some of the traffic being some of the rails that were sold as scrap. A warrant for the abandonment was issued on the 4th July, 1935.

A proposal to close the Sandiacre line in 1937 was made but due to the objections of Imperial Chemical Company who used a considerable amount of water from the canal, the proposal failed, a further proposal in 1943 was also thrown out.

During the years of the Second World War, the canal sections from Swarkestone to Derby and on to Sandiacre did not form part of the main canal network as they did not form part of a through route. When the Transport Act of 1947, an Act which nationalized the great majority of waterways, was being drawn up, the Derby Canal was not included and consequently ownership did not pass to The British Transport Commission and in 1963 to the British Waterways Board.

David Bolton in *Race against Time* mentions a dinner arranged through Peter Scott's influence with Sir Cyril Hurcomb [later Lord Hurcomb], who had been designated to be the first Chairman of the British Transport Commission Robert Aickman asked Sir Cyril why the Derby Canal – one of the few not owned by a railway – had not been brought into the nationalized system since it provided a link between the Trent and Mersey and the Erewash. 'Ah, that was one I managed to miss', replied Hurcomb.

The Derby Canal Company applied for a warrant of abandonment, however Derby Corporation opposed this. The Corporation shortly afterwards changed its mind as it required at least one section in the centre of Derby for road improvement, and they made use of a section for the new road to link Nottingham Road to the Cattle Market before the power of abandonment was granted.

The closure and abandonment was not achieved without a fight. A Restoration Committee was formed in the early 1960s with a view to 'improving and preserving this long line of slumdom', this according to Roy Christian in an article he wrote, 'caused some eyebrows in Derby to rise sharply!'

As mentioned the Derby Corporation had changed their mind and the South East Derbyshire Rural District Council did not wish to see the canal reopened, considering it far to big a task for anyone to tackle. This view prevailed despite the well-publicized fact that the National Trust was at that time starting on the restoration of the Stratford-on-Avon Canal.

The Midlands Branch of the Inland Waterways Association put forward plans for the restoration, but 'road mania' had the last say and the warrant for the abandonment was issued on the 3rd December, 1964.

I had the pleasure of meeting Mr J.R.S. Grimwood-Taylor [the last Clerk to the canal company] shortly afterwards and he said that the members of the company believed that if it had been nationalized, it may have survived, but as a private concern, it did not have the finance to make improvements.

The Derby Canal Co. was wound up on the company's own petition to the High Court in June 1974. As the company had ceased to function as a canal undertaking its remaining assets were transferred to a new holding company, Derby Canal Estates Limited.

The *Derby Evening Telegraph* for 3rd July, 1975 reported:

> The fine warehouses and wharves which had once handled hundreds of thousands of tons of good each year fell gradually into disuse and dereliction. The last pathetic remnants this week falling to the bulldozer and demolition hammer.

The line of the canal is still clear in this photograph taken at Swarkestone Junction looking towards Derby.

Chapter Ten

Revival

Following items on the canal in the local papers etc. during the 1980s, several people began to ask if it would be feasible to re-open the canal for leisure use, say boating and fishing, whilst others could see advantages in providing wild life habitats [this has materialized in part], and as previously mentioned it may resolve drainage problems which occurred after infilling of parts of the canal.

The Derby and Sandiacre Canal Society was formed, its aims are to restore the Derby Canal whereever possible and to provide new sections to link these together so as to form with the Trent and Mersey Canal and the Erewash Canal a 25 mile [40 km] navigable ring. As the original canal corridor into Central Derby was lost under the A52 and industrial development, a new route would be needed; a proposal to make a new section via Pride Park to the Wyvern seems to be an alternative.

In 1993 a restoration report funded by the Southern Derbyshire Training and Enterprise Council was undertaken, its conclusions state:

> Restoration was physically possible,
> It was economically feasible,
> Environmentally desirable.

The Derby and Sandiacre Canal Company was formed in late 1993 and registered as a charity, on doing so it amended its title to the Derby and Sandiacre Canal Trust [Registration Number 1042227].

The *Derby Evening Telegraph* of 8th November, 1994 carried an article on the canal and the trust Chairman, Paul Turner said, 'Derby is one of the few cities that hasn't got its canal back'. The article goes on to say that £13M would be required to re-instate the canal. A feasibility survey followed in 1995 carried out by W.S.Atkins; whilst it confirmed that the restoration was feasible, the cost would however be in the region of £35M.

Work got underway with:

Station Road, and Ullickers bridges at Spondon rebuilt
Swarkestone accommodation bridge restored
Borrowash Bottom lock repairs started
800 yds [730 metres] of canal partly restored [sadly not in water]
Preparation work at Wilmorton with the installation of culverts.
Work to resolve the drainage problems caused by the canal in-filling funded
 in part by Railtrack.

Major works will include crossing under the M1 motorway, a route around a works car park and other commercial developments near the Navigation Inn at Breaston, Also a new bridge is needed on Risley Road, (this could be a lifting bridge similar to the one installed recently on the Rochdale Canal, worked by hydraulic rams to lift the road up when boats wish to pass), and new embankments on several sections. Hard work and money will be needed. The National Heritage Fund will I feel have to step in with some funding before the chugging of boats and the cries of their crews will once more be heard in Derby.

A further hold up I understand is that the entrance to the canal at Sandiacre is privately owned. If this problem could be solved, British Waterways might be persuaded to clear the route as far as the M1, currently a 'moorings for sale' sign stands in the entrance.

The route of National Cycle Network (NCN) 54 follows close to the Little Eaton line for a short distance before it crosses the River Derwent below Darley Abbey. From Derby to Swarkestone, the NCN 6 route is on the canal bed from near Wilmorton College where it passes under the A6 [London Road], then passing several schools and playing fields to Sheldon lock. The edge stones to the lock chamber are visible before the route goes under the A514, this bridge on its under side has murals of the canal. It then cuts alongside a housing estate, where, in several places, the stone towpath edging stones are still *in situ*. Then over Sinfin Moor Lane, the canal went under the lane but the bridge needs considerable work on it. A long is stretch through a 'jungle' which had grown in the canal bed, to which point an attempt was made to clear the channel in the late 1990s. The A50 cuts

Wooden posts mark the position of the chamber of Borrowash top lock.

Looking south, along the cycleway, under the A50 near to the line of the canal. One proposal for restoration is to use this bridge to allow the canal to pass under the road, before it rejoins its old route on Sinfin Moor.

Restored canal bridge at Swarkestone Junction.

through the canal, whilst the cycleway uses an underpass, then a short length on the old towpath to Swarkestone lock, next the NCN crosses over the Trent and Mersey canal and continues via Melbourne, Wilson, Tonge, Worthington to Loughborough and Leicester.

Along the route from Swarkestone to Derby, the East Midlands Electricity Board erected a series of Milestones (made of Iron) with one near the Junction with the Trent and Mersey showing 5 miles to Derby.

At Swarkestone Junction, the lock keeper's house now has a tea room, bed and breakfast facilities.

If you wish to walk this stretch one way, catch a Melbourne bus from the Derby bus station, alight at Cuttle Bridge just prior to Swarkestone, join the Trent and Mersey towpath, under the road and on to the lock. Cross over the canal by the accommodation bridge near the lock keepers house, along the path that bypasses the boat club moorings to join the old canal towpath and then follow the cycle path signs for Derby.

The Derby Canal toll house at Swarkestone Junction.

Top: One of the milestones erected by the East Midlands Electricity Board.

Appendix One

Major Shareholders of the Derby Canal Company

Prior to the first meeting of the Derby Canal Company on the 6th July, 1793, the provisional company held a meeting of the major shareholders on the 11th June, 1793 to elect a committee for the coming year. William Dury Lowe was elected Chairman with Walter Evans as Treasurer; [he was a member of the Evans Family bank in St Mary's Gate].

The major shareholders at this time were:

> Phillip, Earl of Chesterfield, of Bretby Park
> Charles, Earl of Harrington, of Elvaston
> Sir Henry Harpur of Caulke,
> Sir Robert Wilmot of Elveston
> William Drury Lowe of Lockoe

The above were the largest holders of stock, other holders included:

> William Cox, Francis Agard; both corn merchants of Derby
> Thomas and E.W.Cox, wine merchants of Derby
> William Duesbury, manufacturer of 'Crown Derby' china
> Edward Fox, cotton spinner of Derby
> [The Evans family had received £924 from the canal company for
>   their shareholding in the Derwent Navigation]

Several people believe that many of the 'odd decisions' taken by the canal company regarding their refusal on occasions to provide additional lines or facilities to serve local firms and collieries, may have been due to 'self interest' of committee members taking precedence over the commercial activities of the company.

Appendix Two

Castings as ordered by the Company

(Based on the minute books.)

Year	Supplier	Item	Price
1793	Joseph Butler & Co., Chesterfield	Rails	£10 10s. 0d. per ton
1794	ditto	ditto	ditto
1795	Outram & Company	Misc. castings	
1796	Joseph Butler & Co.	Rails	£10 10s. 0d. per ton
1798	Outram & Co.	Wheels	
1799	ditto	20 rails & wheels	£4 9s. 4d.
1804	ditto	Rails	£10 10s. 0d. per ton
	Saxelby & Co., Somercotes	Rails	ditto
1805	ditto	Rails	ditto
1807	ditto	Rails	ditto
1809	Joseph Clayton, Nottingham	Rails	ditto
1814	Saxelby & Co.,	Rails	ditto
	J. & C. Mold, Morley Park	Rails	ditto
1818	ditto	Rails	ditto
1821	J. Harrison, Derby	Ironwork	4d. per pound
	[Gangrails, spikes, lock gate plates, T and L plates, where as screws, bolts above 1 pound each and all other work 6d. per pound]		
1824	J. & C. Mold, Morley Park	Rails	£10 10s. 0d. a ton

Joseph Butler and Co. had been operating a forge at Killamarsh for many years and the district around became known as 'The Forge'.

Outram & Co., Established by Benjamin Outram, William Jessopp, Francis Berresford and John Ridby, in 1790. The name changed to The Butterley Company and by the 1820s was listed as manufacturers of pig, bar, plate, hoop and rod iron and steam engines, with premises at Butterley Park and at Codnor Park. By the 1900s not only had Iron Foundries, but also produced Colliery Plant including headstocks, screening, conveyors and haulage gear. They also had collieries, which produced 4.5 million tons of coal per annum in the 1930s and brickworks with an output of 30 million bricks plus lime & limestone works.

Appendix Three

Costing for the Company and tonnage carried

Labour costs on the various sections – 1806 to 1813

Year	Sandiacre Line	Swarkestone Line	Derwent & Warehouse	Eaton Line	Total
	£	£	£	£	£
1806	106.18	57.40	18.725	84.925	267.23
1807	102.80	26.40	46.00	63.40	239.20
1808	105.66	30.91	31.73	86.74	255.04
1809	85.71	21.95	13.74	71.55	192.95
1810	87.63	50.66	66.95	120.25	325.49
1811	101.85	46.34	19.15	79.90	247.24
1812	202.23	81.38	88.725	73.075	445.41
1813	111.86	103.53	76.12	84.95	376.46
	903.92	418.57	361.74	669.79	2349.02
average	112.99	52.32	45.21	83.72	293.62

These figures are exclusive of lockkeeper's wages or crews for breaking ice.
[Spelling based on an old document kept with the minute books, figures have been converted to pounds and a decimal fraction from £.s.d.].

Statement of the receipts and expenses on the Eaton Line for 1826
Based on old documents kept with the minute books.

Credit	£	Debit	£
W.D.Lowe	1368.35	Eaton Line	152.16
Cash tons	248.35	Railway	86.96
		Taxes on Eaton Line	83.44
		Railway	4.01
		A. Street	48.20
		10 Walls Ho	9.00
		Marfield Road	6.66
		Mr Curzons Salary	20.00
		Do Sarabrough	12.30
		Sundry Salarys	92.48
		John Hoares	18.46
		William Smedly	3.33
	1616.70		736.99

Balance £879.71

The whole length of line is 8 miles 500 yards or 14,580 yards.
[It is apparent that this line was making a profit in 1826.]

Traffic carried on the Canal – for the month of February 1839

Item	Sandiacre Line	Swarkestone Line	Little Eaton Line & Rly.
	tons	tons	tons
Corn	2227 @ 10d.	540 @ 9d.	15 @ 12d.
Coal	1693		3276 @ 3d.
Stone	1135		
Sundries	1752	1919	147 @ 17d.
Chert	113		
Iron Stone	100		
Gravel	182		
Timber	549	15	
Cement	116	520	
Rails	52		
Lead	50	33	
Clay	38	59	
Bricks	60	80	
Totals	82,600	4,209	
Tolls	£344.16	£157.85	

Per Mr Holden	1832
Mr Ray	549
Mr Wooley	967
Mr Broome	71
Denby Old Colly.	157
Total for line	6,252
for a toll of	£270

Sales of coal from Denby Colliery, 1841 – 1846

Period 12 mos to	Sold at Little Eaton Wharf	Openwood Wharf	Smithy Houses & Pottery	Colliery Landsale	Misc.
	tons	tons	tons	tons	tons
1.4.1841	14592	8817	12519	125	
1842	16089	6955.5	13120.5	490	
1843	15264	64099.5*	10996.5	96	
1846	8099.5	653.5+	10113	436.5	108

* and at Belper; + at Belper
Source: the *Drury Lowe Papers*, returns for 1844 & 1845 not available.

Appendix Four

The Openwoodgate Lines
[Also known as the Belper and Morley Park Tramroad]

A series of lines were built over a number a period of 40 years from the Little Eaton Railway to various pits and landsales situated between the railway and Belper. These lines were constructed not by the Derby Canal Company, but by the owners of Denby Colliery and other landowners. It was previously thought that the earliest one was started in 1815, but it is possible that a detached line was built as early as 1806/7. A bed of pot clay was found to underlie a band of soft coal when the Alfreton turnpike (Act 1802, completed 1805) was being made. It was on land owned by William Drury-Lowe of Locko Park and a transcript of an agreement for William Bourne of Belper was made on 14th January, 1806. This agreement was for William Bourne to get 1,000 cubic yards of clay out of a field known as Little Ryefield, the clay to be 'goten' and the field levelled before 25th March, 1813. The Denby pottery was established in 1809, previous to this date the clay went to Belper, the Bourne family carried on potting until 1916, when it was converted into a Limited Company. An oblique reference indicates that a simple tramway was used whilst getting the clay, where it ran is uncertain, this could be the original Belper & Morley tramway mentioned by Farey. In the third volume of his *General view of the Agriculture and Minerals of Derbyshire,* Farey states:

Belper and Morley Park Railway
Since I finished this part of my survey, I have heard that a railway has been laid in the Valley from Belper to Morley Park Collieries, and thence to Denbyhall Colliery

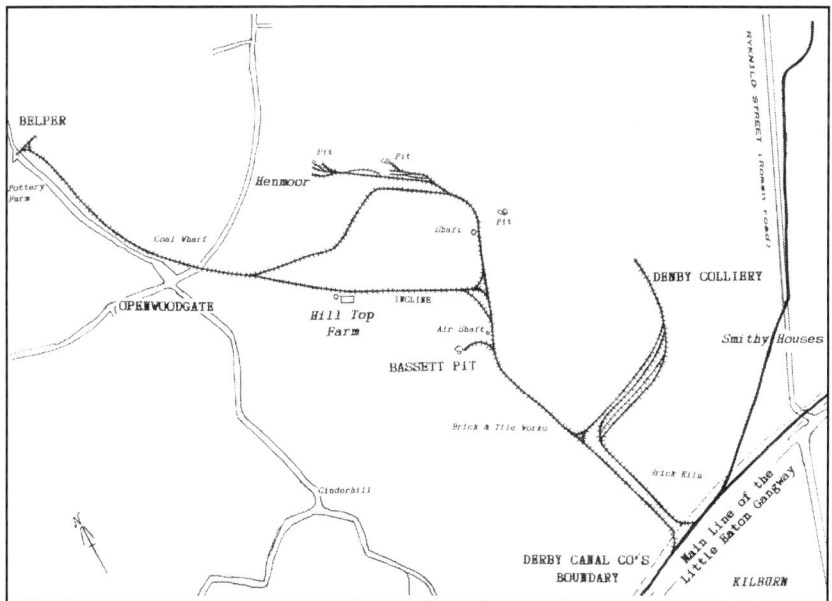

The Openwoodgate lines.

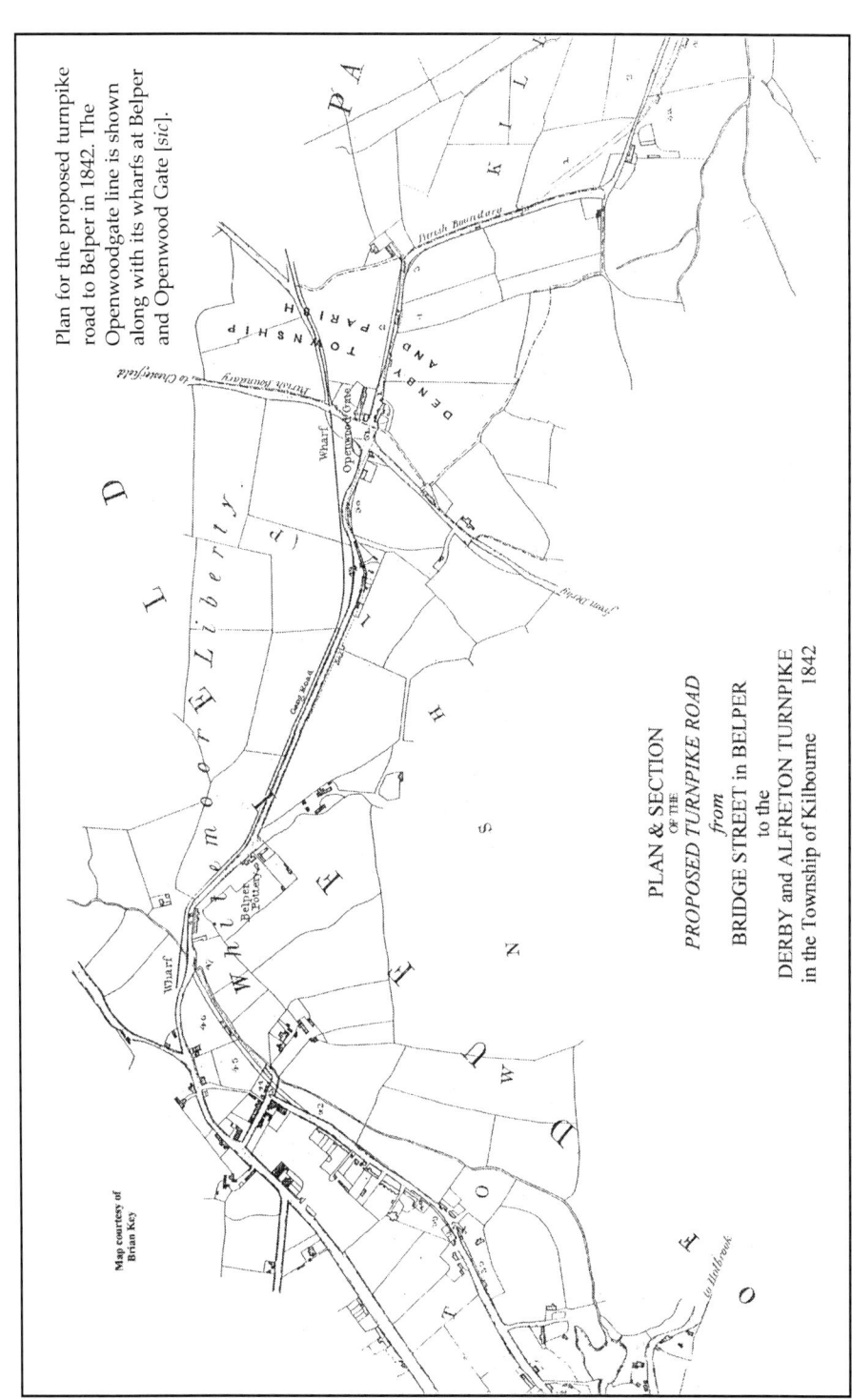

(which also has a Railway to the Derby Canal) a distance of over four miles, for better supplying that large and increasing Town with coals, but I have been disappointed of the levels and other particulars, that I hoped to have received, in time for this account.

At the end to the third volume Farey adds:

After page 313 was in the press, I learned from Mr Charles Sylvester of Derby, who called on me, that another Railway has been made from this colliery, thro' the southern part of Morley-park to Belper Town, see Belper and Morley-Park Railway.

Peter Stevenson remarks in an article that appeared in *Derbyshire Miscellany* in autumn 1973, that this note by Farey is significant, as it shows the close links with the Morley Park Estate.

The late A. Guest in *Changes in the Economic Geography of the Bottle Brook Valley* written as a Thesis in 1968 found the negative attitude of the Derby Canal Company to requests for railway extensions very hard to understand, as mentioned previously their insular attitude no doubt led to the owner of the Denby Colliery, William Drury Lowe, to construct his own lines. As early as 1804, he had had a survey made for a line from his estate into Belper. However a Nail Master of Belper Common delayed the completion of the line to Belper for many years, maybe he had shares in the Alfreton Turnpike Trust.

The route of the first line is not clear, from contemporary maps, the *Drury Lowe Papers* and others held in the Coal Board Archives, a line ran from the Little Eaton Tramway to Henmoor where a land sale wharf was established, this line also served two small pits. The route of this line was still visible in 1970, since then the construction of the A38 dual carriageway has caused major land changes including a landslip near Hill Top Farm. Later the line was extended to Openwoodgate where a land sale wharf was opened to replace the Henmoor Wharf. Coals were then carted down from Openwoodgate to Belper in carts, the charge for this road haulage being 2s. 1d. [10½p] per ton.

On the plan for the proposed Turnpike road from Bridge Street in Belper to the Derby and Alfreton Turnpike at Kilbourne [1842], a gang road is shown running from Hilltop to a wharf at Openwoodgate, then alongside the road to Belper to a wharf near Whitemoor Farm. This wharf is shown on the Woodhouse plan of December 1843 [see sketch overleaf], the edge of the site is occupied by a school erected 1879-80 since replaced by a Sports Hall.

None of the plans show a connection with the Pottery, which was on the opposite side of the road, the pottery would appear to have still been in existence in the latter half of the 19th century as it is clearly marked on the 1884 OS map.

The *Drury Lowe Papers* show the expenses incurred by the Denby Colliery Co. re the 'New Railway' from Openwoodgate to Belper as under:

Year	£	s.	d.
1841	110	17	11
1842	611	3	4
1843	774	16	11
1844	No figures available		
1845	10	9	11½
Total	1507	8	1½

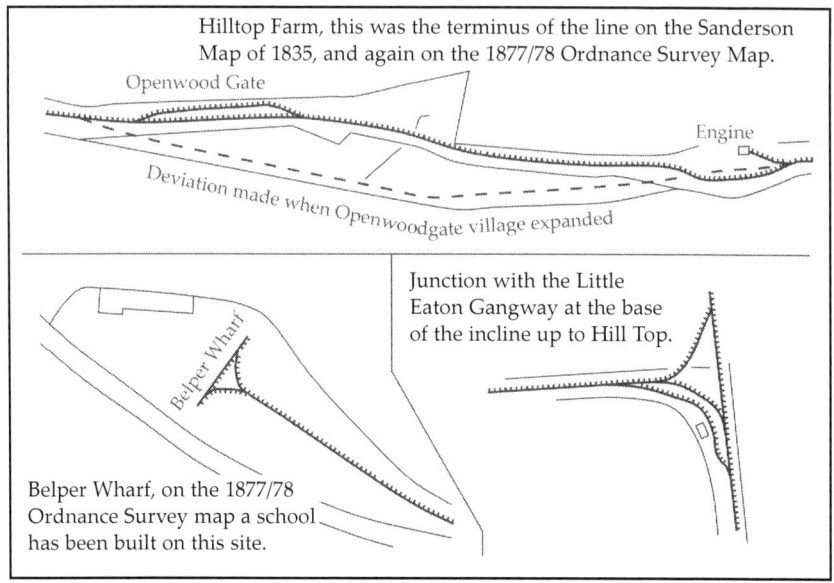

The returns for coal sold by Denby Colliery include in 1843 sales from both Openwoodgate and Belper, whilst those from 1846 show only sales from Belper Wharf.

Sometime prior to the final construction of the line to Belper, several re-alignments had taken place including the installation of a steam winding engine [ex-Morley Park] at Hill Top to work the incline. When the A38 construction caused a land slip, the old winding engine house had to be demolished as were parts of the farm. Whilst the re-building of Hill Top Farm took place several of the stone sleepers and an odd length of rail were found. A wheel pit was located and this sat over a large tank, which had held water for the winding engine.

Of the route that from Belper to Openwoodgate is lost in a housing estate, from Openwoodgate to Hilltop Farm, both a wall and hedge to the side of the farm road mark it, then it passes behind the new farmhouse. Little remains of the incline; if you stand by the Farm and look down you can see where the re-routed footpath meets the line of the old railway, on this section there are some stone sleepers *in situ*, a few with one hole others drilled with two, whilst others lie under the wall.

I was told by an elderly man that lived on Over Lane, that a railway ran from Street Lane past several old coal and ironstone pits to the Stripe; there several branches left the main line, one of which is shown on the 1838 OS map and joins the Hilltop line at the foot of the incline. From the Stripe a line continued past several pits to Henmoor. The 1921 OS map shows this route as footpath, with several old pits still marked near to its route, it also continued across Over Lane near Whitemoor House to near Whitemoor Farm. Could this have been an early line to Belper?

Several wharves, lines and deviations are shown on the Woodhouse plans, Sandersons map and the various OS maps [*see sketches*]. This series of lines may never be fully explained as many were to serve pits whilst in production and then removed or re-located when the pits were worked out.

THE OPENWOOD GATE LINES

Bridge over the A38 which is on the route of the line. The stone sleepers can be found along the wall on the far side of the bridge.

Left: The line ran along this wall from Hill Top Farm towards Openwoodgate. *Right*: looking up the incline to Hill Top Farm, in the bottom right corner one of the stone sleepers is visible in the road.

Aerial photograph of Hill Top Farm in the 1960s. The Openwoodgate line ran along the wall across the centre of the picture.

Several small lines ran from the gangway. The route of one of these to a number of coal pits in Openwoodgate follows the line of trees in the centre photograph. In the lower photograph the site of a tile works, served by one of the lines, could still be seen in the 1990s.

Appendix Five

Report from George Stephenson
To the Committee of the Derby Canal Company

Gentlemen,

In compliance with your instructions, I have examined the Little Eaton Branch of the Derby Canal together with the Railway laid up to Smithy Houses for the purpose of ascertaining the practicability of converting the Canal into a Railway and generally of ascertaining what improvements can be made in the whole line of communications between the Collieries and Denby to render it impossible for the Turnpike road to compete with the Railway in the transit of coal.

There are two modes in which I conceive this may be effected. One is the adoption of the present lines on which new rails should be laid down and some of the most objectionable Curves done away with. The other consists of taking an entirely new Line. The latter course I prefer not only because a much better communication would be obtained but because I believe a new line may be made at a less cost than the necessary improvements in the old Line exclusive of the cost of Land. By adopting a New Line the transit of coals would be continued along the old line until the new one was finished. Whereas the Carriage upon the old line must be entirely suspended whilst undergoing the requisite alterations.

I subjoin an Estimate of the probable Cost of Executing the proposed alterations in the old Line and of forming the new one.

Estimate of Old Line

	£
Iron Rails, 35 lb to the yard = 55 tons for 8 miles = tons @ £10	4,400
Chairs	1,466
Keys, pins, plugs etc.	388
Stone Blocks and Sleepers at 1s. 6d. each	2,112
Laying and Ballasting the way at 3s. per linear yard	2,112
	10,478
Cutting and embankment required on the Old Line including Alterations in Bridges etc.	3,200
	13,678
Contingencies at 10 per cent	1,367
	15,045
Deduct price of Old Cast Iron Rails at £4 per ton	1,760
Total Cost	£13,285

Estimate for New Line

	£
Rails, chairs, etc., Stone Blocks & Sleepers, laying and Ballasting The way as per the foregoing Estimate	10,478
Cuttings and embankments £200 per mile	1,760
Fencing at 2s. per yard	1,408
	13,646
Contingencies at 10 per cent	1,364
	15,010
deduct for old Cast Iron Rails at £4 per ton	1,760
Total cost of new line	£13,250

Side view of one of the waggons, May 1947.   *H. Murray / A. Rimmer Collection*

Appendix Six

The Derby Canal

(As given in *Bradshaw's Canals and Navigable Rivers of England and Wales*, edited by Henry de Salis, 1st edition, 1904)

Short Description

The canal commences at Sandiacre by a junction with the Erewash Canal and proceeds by Borrowash and Spondon to Derby, where there are junctions with the Little Eaton branch and a short branch to the upper section of the River Derwent in the town. At Derby the canal crosses the River Derwent on the level between White Bear Lock and Pegg's Flood Lock, and continues by Osmaston and near Chellaston to Swarkestone, where it forms a junction with the Trent and Mersey Canal.

The branch to Little Eaton communicates at Little Eaton with a tramway four miles in length to Kilbourne and Denby.

The whole course of the Canal is in the county of Derbyshire.

Proprietors, Officers and Offices

The Derby Canal Company
Manager: Sidney Burton
Office: Cockpit Hill Wharf, Derby

Distance Table
Main Line (No.27a)

Sandiacre Junction, junction with Erewash Canal (No 30) to:	Miles	Furlongs
Breaston	1	7
Borrowash Top Lock & Railway Station	4	7
Spondon Railway Station	6	1
Derby, junction with Little Eaton Branch (No 27b)	8	6
Derby, junction with branch to upper portion of River Derwent (No. 27c)	9	0
Derby, White Beat Lock	9	1
Derby, Pegg's Lock	9	1½
Derby, Gandy's Wharf	9	2
Derby, Gas Works	10	2
Osmaston	11	0
Shelton Top Lock	13	0
Baltimore Bridge, Chellaston	13	4
Swarkestone (Junction with Trent and Mersey Canal Main Line (No. 76a)	14	4

Little Eaton Branch (No.27b)

Derby, junction with Main Line (No.27a) to:	Miles	Furlongs
Depot Lock		5
Little Chester	6	
Eaton Top Lock	1	2
Ford Farm	2	3
Little Eaton, termination of Canal and Railway Station	3	1

	Miles	Furlongs
Branch to upper portion of River Derwent (No.27c)		
Junction with Main Line (No. 27a) to:		
Phoenix Lock	½	
Junction with River Derwent	1	
G.N. Railway Bridge, River Derwent, termination of Navigation	2	

Locks

Main Line (No.27a)

1 and 2 Sandiacre
3 and 4 Borrowash

Rise to Derby

5 White Bear

Fall to River Derwent, Derby

6 Pegg's Flood Lock
7 Day's

Rise from River Derwent to Gandy's Wharf, Derby

8 and 9 Shelton

Fall to Swarkestone

Little Eaton Branch (no.27b)

1 Pasture
2 Depot
3 Sharon
4 Eaton Top

Rises to Little Eaton

Branch to upper portion of River Derwent, Derby, (No. 27c)

1 Phoenix

Maximum size of vessels that can use the navigation

		Feet	inches
Length		72	0
Width		14	0
Draught	3 feet to	3	8
Headroom		7	0

Types of vessels using the navigation: Narrow boats and Upper Trent Boats.

Towing Path

There is a towing-path throughout the navigation with the exception of the branch to the upper portion of the River Derwent, Derby.

Appendix Seven

Bylaws
Extracts from the Minute Books.

Made 21st June, 1795
Each up-gate carriage on meeting another on the railway shall give way and turn off the road at the nearest passing place so as not to obstruct or hinder the down-gate carriage or the person having the care of such up-gate carriage, shall for every such offence forfeit a sum not exceeding twenty shillings.

Made 1800
Persons may drive horses and cattle along the railway. Horses to pay 1d. each and cattle ½d. for liberty of passing along each railway branch.

Made 12th December, 1803
If the driver of any gang of coals turns out of the road except for an accident, he shall forfeit 5s. for each offence.

If the driver of an empty Waggon or gang meets a loaded Waggon or gang between two meeting places, the empty Waggon shall be drawn back to the next meeting place as soon as possible or forfeit 5s.

If any loaded Waggon or cart shall be driven over the railroad on to the Wharf at Eaton, the driver shall forfeit 2s. 6d.

Acknowledgements

The Derby City Local Studies Staff; The Derbyshire County Library Service; Mr Terry Judge; Mrs E. M. Guest for permission to use extracts from the Thesis by the late A.Guest; Mr Peter Stevenson; Mr Ron Vickers; Taylor, Simpson and Mosley, Solicitors for permission to use extracts from the Derby Canal Company Papers; Mrs Ann Priestley; Mrs E. M. Bishop; Mr E. H. Kitchen; Mr A. Savage; Mr Alan Jeffreys and various members of the Derby and Sandiacre Canal Society; Sustrans for allowing reproduction of parts of the National Cycle Network Guides; the drivers of Trent & Barton Bus who have told me how to get to various points and more important, told me how to get back; and special thank you to all that have written, phoned with information, or have guided me on the right track on my frequent trips around Derby.

Bibliography

Baxter, Bertram. *Stone Blocks and Iron Rails*, 1966
Brewster, [Ed], *Edinburgh Encyclopaedia*, 1830
Burton, Anthony, *The Great Days of the Canals*, 1989
Carter, E. F. *Railway Encyclopaedia*, 1963
Calvert, Roger, *Inland Waterways of Britain*, 1963
Dendy Marshall, C. F. *History of British Railways down to the Year 1840*, 1938
Edwards, K. C. [Ed], *Nottingham and its Region*, 1966
Farey, John, *Agriculture and Minerals of Derbyshire*, 3 vols, 1817
Fryar, Mark, *Some chapters in the history of Denby*, 1934
Hadfield, C., *The Canal Age*, 1966
Hadfield, C., *The Canals of the East Midlands*, 1968
Lee, C.E. *The Evolution of Railways*, 2nd Edn. 1943
Macauley John [Ed], *Modern Railway Working*, Vol. 1, 1912
Nixon, Frank, *Notes on the Engineering History of Derbyshire*, 1955
Nixon, Frank, *Industrial Archaeology of Derbyshire*, 1969
Phillips, J., *History of Inland Navigation*, 1795
Potter, Eric, In search of Outram's Railway, *Ad Rem*, 1953
Priestley, Joseph, *Historical Account of the Navigable Rivers, Canals and Railways throughout Great Britain*, 1831. Reprint 1969 by David & Charles
Rees, Adam, *Cyclopedia*, 1808/14
Russell, Ronald, *Lost Canals of England and Wales*, 1971
Scott, Highland, *Transactions*, 1824
Smyth. W.W. *The Iron Ores of Great Britain*, 1886
Stevenson, Robert, *Highland Essays*, 1824
Ward, J., *Pleasant Rambles around Derby*, 1895
Williams, F.S., *Iron Roads*, 5th Edn. 1884
Williams. J.E., *The Derbyshire Miners*, 1962
Various editions of the Bulmer, Kelly, White, and Pigot series of Directories of Derbyshire.

Magazines, Society Journals and Transactions include:

Ad Rem (magazine of the Butterley Company, Derby)
Journals of the Derbyshire Archaeological Society
Derbyshire Miscellany
Onwards (journal of the IWPS)
Derbyshire Countryside
Newcome Society Transactions
Country Life
The Derby Mercury – 1790 to 1830
Derbyshire Evening Telegraph
The Derby Trader
Journal of the Railway and Canal Historical Society